PRAISE FOR THE FASTLANE TO BUILDING RELATIONSHIPS

"In *The Fastlane to Building Relationships,* Christian takes the reader through the blueprint of how he created his own social ecosystem. From the Central California coast to the "hotbed" of Newport Beach with all its glitz and glamor, Christian walks you through his process step by step. What is so enjoyable about this game-changing book is I have a front row seat to watch him put his writing in action. Christian has supported the SUP Vets Foundation, attended a retreat, and hosted an event where our organization was able to present and raise capital, and he continually refers amazing people to me on almost a weekly basis. This book is alive. Christian is living it every day. Follow him on social media, attend one of his events, and you'll discover a genuine human who cares and has found his passion at the intersection of people and business. Having been in the business development world for my entire career post Navy, I can tell you this book is well worth your time. I plan on sending it to my children as they prepare and continue to navigate their nascent business careers. He's obviously a student of some of the masters in NLP, sales strategies, and networking. This book is a summary of their teachings and a personal testimony to how Christian made these teachings his own, defied human nature, and did the work to create an amazing and powerful network in minimal time."

—*James Bartelloni, Former Top Gun & Founder of The SUP Veterans*

"I wish *The Fastlane to Building Relationships* was around when I was in college. Networking is usually an amorphous concept that people know they need to do, but never have explained to them. This book fills the gap. Christian synthesizes the most useful concepts in sales, business, and social psychology to create an actionable plan to succeed in building relationships and gaining standing in your local community."

—*Nick Pardini, Founder of Davos Investment Group*

"*The Fastlane to Building Relationships* is a comprehensive, practical guide that offers insightful strategies for cultivating connections in personal, professional, and digital contexts. The narrative style is accessible and engaging, presenting theories as actionable advice that can genuinely enhance relationship-building efforts. White emphasizes the significance of hosting events, reframing it as a strategy that anyone can utilize to foster relationships, regardless of scale. The book stands out for its holistic approach, covering various aspects of relationships and equipping readers to thrive in a fast-paced, interconnected world."

—*Danielle Sprouls, Esq.*

"If there's anyone to learn the process of building social capital from, then you'd be hard pressed to find anyone smarter than Christian. It's impressive with the community he's been able to build in Southern California and the relationships he's helped me cultivate along with countless others. He's truly someone exciting to be around and if I were you, I'd be motivated to learn as much as possible from him!"

—*Alec Mountain, Entrepreneur*

THE FASTLANE TO BUILDING RELATIONSHIPS

The Art of Curating a Social Ecosystem

Christian E. White

CEW Publishing

ISBN: 979-8-9887818-1-3

I dedicate this book to my parents,
Monique and Stewart.

ACKNOWLEDGEMENTS

First, I would like to thank my family, especially my parents, for everything they've done for me over the years.

Thank you, James Bartelloni, Danielle Sprouls, Sanaz Abravani, and Nick Pardini for their invaluable input on this book.

I would also like to acknowledge those who have helped me in my professional career, including Paul Pena, Joseph Martin, Carl Sims, Rudy Blakenship, John Nipp, and Terri Giovacchini.

Thank you to Kyle and Garrett Hicks, Shylean Garcia, Shayan Zoghi, Brad Huxley, Brian Furstenfeld, Craig Elester, Derek Bredefeld, Cherelle Reaves-Berrard, Dylan Wilson, Jacob Mooradian, Iliana Duarte, Griffin Raphael, Kristy Olson, Landon Domenico, Brion Ballman, Conrad Cione, Mike Orzell, Jules Wilson, Anthony Cecere, Mike Sanchez, Gail Thackray, Jeff Reisner, Bill Lobel, Deborah Donahue and Pouya Hashemi for your help and inspiration to create a social ecosystem.

I would also like to acknowledge all those who have served and continue to serve and protect this great nation.

Finally, thank you to everyone who has shaped me into the man I am today, especially those I attended school with and served alongside in the Navy. Were it not for you, coupled with the challenges I've encountered over the years, I wouldn't be half the man I am today.

CONTENTS

INTRODUCTION

"A journey of a thousand miles
begins with a single step."
—Lao Tzu

My aim in writing this book is to share with you the tools that have enabled me to build authentic relationships, both personally and professionally. I'm confident that this information will help you foster relationships that will lead to friends, clients or customers, enhancing both the quality of your life and your success at whatever it is that you do. I don't think of myself as some guru, but what I can tell you—with certainty—is that I know a thing or two about people. And this book seeks to distill in as short a read as possible the most important points and ideas that I've found critical to establishing and building relationships. I don't know about you, but I've always wished there was one source to go to on any given topic, instead of having to read a plethora of sources and piece them all together. I want this book to serve as exactly that: an amalgamation. The information I

1

share with you is germane to all relationships, be they for business, personal or romantic purposes. I'll also share with you creative ways to get in front of people and how to leverage your skill sets so you can cruise in the fast lane. As needed, I'll endeavor to update this book from time to time.

I believe that EQ (emotional quotient) is not covered enough in academia, nor is it fully appreciated by society. Moreover, I find it fascinating that in many organizations, from private companies to governmental organizations, how many people are socially incompetent. This can lead to an array of challenges for the entire organization, from feelings of not being heard and understood to feeling slighted for things that could have been handled more tactfully. There are, of course, a plethora of books on how to build better relationships. My goal is to provide you with new content, while at the same time underscoring classic foundational elements, because, in the words of Zig Ziglar, "Repetition is the mother of learning, the father of action, which makes it the architect of accomplishment." It's striking to me how many people do things that alienate themselves from others—or leave money on the table, literally and/or figuratively, in their interactions with others. Examples include the neighbor with a grievance, or the person who uses poor negotiating skills with their spouse. This book will help you become aware of these alienating behaviors so you can enhance your interpersonal skills. While I can't guarantee that every technique on these pages will work for everyone, I can tell you that if you apply these principles, you'll experience an improvement on some level that may make all the difference for your business or personal life. And if you can take away and apply at least one piece of information from this book, then I'll feel I've done my job.

Because even tiny, incremental improvements in the sphere of relationships will compound towards higher and higher levels of self-actualization. Over the years, I've been able to meet billionaires, celebrities and fascinating people of all backgrounds and walks of life by applying the knowledge you're about to read. Despite what the media would have you believe, now is the greatest time to be alive, and our access to both people and resources is unparalleled by any other period in human history. At the same time, despite the level of connectivity that the internet and social media have brought us, society is more deprived of deep relationships than at any other time in history. This is due to a combination of factors, including both the digitalization of society and the decline of traditional institutions like religion. Despite this we, as a society, still crave for such relationships, stemming from our innate desire to emotionally connect. As the world continues to evolve around us and technology advances—particularly artificial intelligence—there will always be a tremendous demand for human interaction on a deeper level. I'll also share with you how I was able to establish myself in one of the most competitive places in the world, Southern California, in less than a year—and how I was able to create more relationships than I had previously created in any other year of my life. I'll show you step by step how to replicate this yourself, and how to do it efficiently by leveraging others with complementary skills. Building relationships is a skill, and like any skill, it can be learned. Naturally, extroverts will have an advantage; however, by consistently applying the information in this book, everyone can achieve improvement. Most importantly, the relationships we have with our parents, family and friends are at the heart of what drives us. And its relationships that help you secure that career opportunity that others haven't seen advertised, that allows for a warm introduction to that person you like, and that, when you face hard times or need extra support, provide you the means to overcome those challenges. As you might expect, those who are rich in relationships are better hedged against unwelcome events and are better positioned to navigate obstacles more effectively. Not having a team supporting you can be catastrophic both personally and professionally. In this book I've referenced several great published works and people from whom I've learned valuable lessons from over the years. No one is truly self-made; each of us has been guided by various individuals and opportunities throughout our lives.

If you're tight on time or wish to absorb only the key points, then feel free to skip to parts of the book that pertain to you— then be sure to come back and reread the book for better retention. I'll also mention that these are my actual words; I did not have a ghostwriter, nor did I rely on AI or any other means to write this book. Finally, if you already consider yourself an expert in relationships, then I encourage you to jump straight to the chapter about hosting curated social gatherings.

CHAPTER 1

MY JOURNEY

"Even the darkest night will
end and the sun will rise."
—Victor Hugo

Most people who know me today would be surprised to learn that I really did not have much of a social life growing up. In fact, I grew up in a home where neither socializing nor team-based sports were prioritized. Which naturally led to a lack of affinity for playing sports like football or basketball. As you can imagine, a kid who lacks social skills, coupled with the inability to play sports that his classmates are engaged with at lunchtime and after school, is setting himself up for ostracism.

This, in addition to anxiety and the inability to focus, was an absolute disaster for me. I recall at times being quite distant from others my age and feeling so isolated that I went to great lengths to conceal my lack of friends. To eat up time, I would intentionally stand in the longest lines to grab lunch. When I did hang out with others, they were often people who didn't share my same views or values— just for the sake of company. More often, I found myself resorting to spending lunchtimes at the nurse's or teacher's office. Eventually, after I struggled personally, socially and academically for years, my parents recognized that traditional school was not working out. And following my freshman year of high school, they enrolled me in an online school.

Those years between the ages of 10 to 16 were not very enjoyable. And I had no one to blame but myself. It wasn't until my first year of college that I really began to open up socially.

For me, skipping the typical high school experience and reemerging for college life required that I adapt and learn quickly.

And if having to catch up socially in college was a challenge, joining the Navy upon graduation was even more so— particularly its special warfare selection program. Aside from its mentally and physically demanding tasks (which, of course, were intended to get you to quit), being in a competitive program presented social challenges as well. I quickly learned the selection course I was in was unlike any form of band of brother-like environment, which is often romanticized in novels and the media. I witnessed and experienced firsthand the vitriol and dog-eat-dog nature of people vying for a spot in a competitive program. I also observed the politics and favoritism that permeated the training pipeline I was in as well. While this career path I'd been pursuing and investing in for several years didn't materialize, I walked away with considerable experience humbled, yet fiercely driven. I used to fantasize about going back in time and doing things differently, crushing it this time; however, I now realize I have a different purpose in life and there's no value in ruminating on the past. I've instead chosen to harness any pain, resentment and emotions towards other ambitions. It's even been cathartic to revisit these memories and write about them. (Sidenote: It's never good to keep things bottled up, because they *will* manifest in other areas in your life. If need be, I recommend talking it out with someone or writing out your thoughts.

All of this means that I've been able to learn a thing or two about building relationships, both personally and professionally. I've also learned a lot from various authors (see the appendix for a list of books I recommend you read) and from trial and error, including cold calls, knocking on doors and cold approaches. Been there, done that, got the T-shirt.

I've always believed in starting with the fundamentals, so that's what we'll do beginning in the next chapter. Again, if any of this feels redundant, feel free to skip around to the parts of this book that speak to you. That said, I still believe there's value in revisiting these fundamentals, as we often need information reinforced for retainment.

CHAPTER 2

THE BASICS

"The mind and body are not separate.
What affects one affects the others."
—Casio Jones

Many readers will know, but it bears repeating, that if you don't have a solid foundation mentally and physically, then you're inhibiting yourself. I say this from experience: it's not fun, and it can drastically limit your potential. Be sure you're taking care of your mind and body through proper nourishment, programming and exercise.

Starting in the mid-20th century, much research has been done on the subject of psychosomatics (psycho, pertaining to the mind, and somatics, pertaining to the body). This is also known as the mind-body connection, and a key finding of this field is that the stressors of life can manifest in various ways—both physical, in the form of pain, think back pain, and mental, in the form of anxiety disorders, depression and migraines. The more we're aware of this correlation, the better we'll be at identifying the source and bringing balance to our lives if things are out of whack.

Sidenote: I'm obviously not a physician, nor do I purport to be any kind of health expert, but I can tell you with absolute certainty that there is indeed a mind-body connection.

I used to deal with chronic pain, and it wasn't until I came across the field of psychosomatics that I recognized the link between the ailments that affect everyday people and the stressors of life. Being perfectionistic, self-critical or in a stressful environment over time can lead to a variety of health challenges that can only be remedied through bringing about balance in your life. Be sure to take rest and take care of both your mind and body. Don't make the mistake I made of buying into the narrative that you must work 80+ hours a for months or years to be successful. After all, there's a price for everything. I wish I had taken more time to relax, enjoy the moment and relish the time I spent with family and friends.

If someone tells you that you need to continually put in superhuman work hours to achieve success for many months or years—I encourage you to ask them about their mental and physical health, relationships, or quality of life. Of course, we're all different, and for some, working an exorbitant number of hours may be the price they wish to pay, while for others it's the ninth circle of hell.

And yes, there will be times in life when you find yourself burning the metaphorical candle at every possible end; however, you can still find space to rest your body and mind. Just like going to the gym, you must rest. And never feel guilty for taking a break. Early in my career, I thought I wasn't supposed to take any time off, but I was wrong. I believe you *can* achieve greatness in life while maintaining a modicum of balance. You are your greatest asset, so never stop investing in yourself—mentally and physically.

Additionally, I suggest incorporating affirmations into your daily routine, if you aren't doing so already. These are incredibly potent when done consistently over time, and they complement the work you are putting in each day. Whether you believe in God or the universe, —what we say and focus on, we draw into our lives, period. That's why I strive to focus all my energy and attention on what I want to bring about. There's already enough focus in the world on things that aren't productive to society.

Challenges

If you're experiencing major hurdles at this point in your life, know that you're never alone. As dark as things may be for you, remember, in the words of Victor Hugo, *"Even the darkest night will end, and the sun will rise."* I've been there, too; I've had some very difficult times, whether it was in school growing up and feeling completely lost or falling

12

short of career ambitions. I know what it's like to feel like you've been punched in the gut and you're struggling to get up. Ultimately, the key to overcoming these hurdles is to reach out to others who've been in similar situations, or who are where we want to be ourselves.

If you aren't happy with where you are in life, then you're doing something wrong. Remember, there are *literally* millions of people around the world who would kill to have even a fraction of the things you have and have experienced. I have to remind myself of this whenever I personally deviate.

Daily Regimen

"Imagination rules the world." — Napoleon Bonaparte

Visualization – Ideally, you do this every morning as soon as you wake up, and when you go to bed, as it facilitates mental programming while you sleep. I also highly recommend imagining the *feeling* of already possessing whatever it is you desire; not just imagining a new house, car, etc., but truly engaging with the emotions associated with already having what you seek. Personally, I enjoy listening to music at various frequencies while I visualize. These frequencies can be 432hz or 963hz, etc.

Dietary Supplements – For those of you inclined, or without proper nutrition, I suggest incorporating natural supplements into your morning routine.

Affirmations – Affirmations are words and thoughts that we can utilize to program a positive mindset. These absolutely work when *done* in conjunction with *taking action.*

"What we focus on expands." — Tony Robbins

Incorporating these exercises daily, coupled with taking *thoughtful, consistent action*, will increase the likelihood of you accomplishing your objectives.

Character

"So much depends on reputation – guard it with your life." — Robert Greene

It's easy to forget how big of an impact our reputation has on our lives and opportunities. The truth is, failure to accurately understand how you're received by others can cost you dearly. It's our character and the reputation we have that can make or break us, so don't leave this to chance. Clearly, nobody is perfect, striving to embody virtues such as integrity, humility and consideration of others will pay dividends. To borrow the wise words from John Wooden, *"Be more concerned with your character than your reputation, because your character is what you really are, while your reputation is merely what others think you are."*

Also, remember that you're always being watched, whether you're aware of it or not, whether it's the man or woman

14

next to you or the myriad of technological devices that monitor our daily lives.

Embracing Obstacles

At any time you can divorce yourself of any issue that's afflicting you (although this is easier said than done). People tend to ruminate and subject themselves to emotional distress over things that they have little to no control over. We must remember that everything is a matter of perception and that we hold more power within ourselves than we realize. As they say, *"You don't know what you don't know."*

Life becomes easier when we embrace the imperfections of daily life—schedules not being exactly right, people deviating, and events outside of our control. We should recognize and accept these circumstances—but our focus should be on identifying the *solution* as opposed to the *problem*.

Nobody is perfect, and buying into the notion that we can be just sets us up for disappointment. If something happens, take ownership of it; then do your best to make it right and move on. Considering scenarios where we may drop the ball, what matters is how we respond and how we seek to make amends.

Synergy

It is essential that, whenever you're a part of a team, that you add value. And if you ever notice yourself not keeping up, you need to recognize it, and either step up or dismiss yourself from the team. Nothing breeds animosity more than when someone else is carrying another person's weight.

I've observed this take place, especially in military training, where those who failed to keep up were systematically purged by the group via ostracism or physical attacks. Don't just pull your weight, be invaluable to your team. Not only will your team appreciate you more, but you're better protected within the group—especially if it's at work, as you'll have better job security and other benefits.

The following points are from Robert Greene's book, *The 48 Laws of Power,* and are important reminders as you work with others:

- **Never appear too perfect** – People tend to envy those who give the perception that everything is wonderful in their lives.
- **Never outshine the master** – Whether this is your boss or manager, be careful to not make them feel threatened.
- **Don't build fortresses to protect yourself; isolation is dangerous** – Think of any scenario where you're

sequestered from others. Failure to stay abreast of key information and the ability to bond with colleagues, clients and people in general, can lead to disastrous consequences for yourself or others.

Tip: Aside from simply doing your job well and helping others excel at theirs, there are a multitude of ways in which you can add value. Even simple things like bringing coffee, pastries, or your sense of humor to work can go a long way towards boosting morale.

Optics

"For the great majority of mankind are satisfied with appearances, as though they were realities, and are often more influenced by the things that seem than by those that are." – Niccolò Machiavelli

There's an adage I learned years ago in the Navy—*perception is reality*—and I've often found it to be true. I would also like to add that you must tailor your image to your target audience. If you're in tech, then sport a tech look; if you're in the music industry, then dress and look the part of a musician.

We've all heard the adage *"dress for success."* In today's culture, where the casual look has become more and more the norm, looking sharp still holds a great deal of weight. It can even mean the difference between someone taking you seriously, and giving you their time, or completely blowing you off. Things like what we wear can send signals regarding our socioeconomic status and competency. Our perceived attractiveness—not to include physical looks, will either improve or diminish our standing. When you meet up in person with someone, they have already distilled an impression of you, before you even utter a word.

There's a reason designers spend considerable time on book covers, movie covers, and, for social media content creators, thumbnails. It's because people decide within seconds whether they want to engage with content based on how it looks.

Never forget that. And you never know who you may run into when you're out and about, even at the grocery store. This is especially important if you're in a profession like real estate where anyone could potentially be a client or customer.

The same is true of your vehicle; it's an extension of you, so make sure it looks sharp and is clean and presentable.

If you look sharp every day, the compliments you receive will add up, and not only positively impact you, but those around you (remember, someone is always watching). We can all recall a time when we were complimented and it boosted our self-esteem, motivating us and improving our mood. We live in a highly competitive world, so do everything you can to give yourself an edge. Take charge of your image, and cultivate one that matches the person you wish to become. Just like your reputation, don't leave this up to chance; get in and remain in the driver's seat.

I personally enjoy wearing blazers, for two reasons: first, who doesn't like the look? I mean, they look good when smartly worn, and second, the blazer exudes professionalism and therefore competency.

Even if you wear a T-shirt underneath, with jeans and a pair of sneakers, it can go a long way towards enhancing your presentation. Hence why, if you were to run into me, nine times out of ten you would see me in a blazer.

Ladies—I recommend wearing the equivalent of a blazer.

People like to associate with people who look and act like them. Humans are naturally tribal, which partly explains why we tend to segregate ourselves into regions, neighborhoods, and even businesses with others who share our background, whether this is cultural, political or socio-economic.

Historically, people in positions of power have always had a distinct look and/or attire. It serves as a symbol of their authority and denotes their role. Now, dressing sharp and looking professional doesn't mean you have to wear a suit or blazer Monday through Friday; however, at the very least, wearing even something as simple as a collared shirt can enhance the way you feel and how you're received.

Looking sharp each day can go a very long way towards building your brand and leveling up your personal and professional life. Remember, the little things add up. That person at the door of some event will receive you differently when you look on point than the individual who's casually dressed. I've even seen a professionally dressed person walk up to a specific department in a store, where there was already a group of people waiting for an employee, only for that employee—not knowing who had been waiting first—immediately focus on helping the professionally dressed person over the others.

Our third president, Thomas Jefferson, was known for his underdressed appearance, with some visitors mistaking him for a servant. One notable visitor even felt slighted by his unprofessional appearance. Jefferson's understated look served neither him nor the country in these encounters. The clothing you wear can either make or break you and can be successfully leveraged to influence.

Personal Brand

Our personal brand is a blend between our character and our appearance, ultimately crafting the way in which we're received by others. What's your personal brand? Are you a brand that's trusted and reliable and that looks put together, or one that's unreliable and to be avoided? Do you want to be the brand-new Rolls Royce or the beat-up 25-

year-old Ford Fiesta with the squeaky belt? If need be, ask friends or family for feedback on how you present yourself.

Next, ask yourself how you want to be perceived by others. People don't have the time, nor even the desire in many cases, to delve into who we are as people and are thus reliant upon their senses to determine who we are. Your word choice, tone, inflection and cadence can all convey your background, whether it's via phone or meeting in person. Are you a reflection of the type of person you wish to become and associate with?

That's why you must be thoughtful of your brand. Don't leave it to chance; take charge of how you present yourself to others.

It's equally important to have a presentable vehicle and office.

The People We Associate With

Each person we choose to surround ourselves with inevitably influences the course of our lives. We've all had parents or educators caution us against mingling with specific individuals or groups. The saying that we become the average of our associates holds true in most cases.

I've frequently pondered a person's willingness to connect with others, especially those of lower socioeconomic status or from a different group, as a measure of their self-assuredness. To illustrate, someone who's already highly regarded by their peers due to their influence is not diminished by associating with those that others deem less worthy of consideration.

However, the person lacking social clout who interacts with those of perceived lesser value may stand to lose the social capital they may have otherwise built with either their peers or those of greater clout.

I've observed this; however, it's typically not overt, but conveyed in an indirect manner. This is something to be cognizant of as you engage with others.

The Variables of Success

Everyone is looking for the secret to success in their personal and/or work life. I see success as the culmination of several factors, but most important among them is an insatiable *desire* to succeed. Without this desire, there's nothing motivating us to work that extra hour, read, study, or labor through trials and tribulations. It's indeed desire that serves as the catalyst for those that have achieved greatness in life.

Motivation aside, there are certainly additional ingredients to success, ranging from the family we're born into and our socioeconomic status to our culture, personality, politics, and more.

We're all dealt a deck of cards in life, which we have to make the most of in our lifetime. While I wish I could say otherwise, life is inherently unfair. But we can *create* our fortune by working smart and industriously, positioning ourselves wisely, receiving mentorship and increasing our surface area for luck.

Remember, people like people who look, act, talk, and sound just like them. Whichever path you're pursuing, you must, to at least some degree, ingratiate yourself with the people you wish to become. Sometimes we aren't always aware of how we're conducting ourselves, so I encourage you to ask the trusted individuals in your life to provide genuine feedback.

Age

Age is less of a determiner of success than you might think. There have been a great many people who have achieved greatness both at an early age and later in life. For example, Napoleon was about 31 years of age when he became the leader of France following a coup d'état. Alexander the Great became king at the age of 18, whereupon he began expanding his territory and had conquered most of the known world by age 30. Over a thousand years later, Joan of Arc was 17 years old when she contributed militarily to France's cause during the Hundred Years War.

Conversely, there have been many who have enjoyed success later in life, including Stan Lee, who created Marvel Comics. Lee only began to experience great success when he reached about 40 years of age. The famous cook Julia Child didn't achieve fame until even later in life, in her 50s. The man behind McDonalds, Ray Kroc, met success in his early 50s, and Kentucky Fried Chicken's Colonel Sanders didn't rise to prominence until he reached his 60s.

Environment

> *"You are a product of your environment. So, choose the*
> *environment that will best develop you toward your objective.*
> *Analyze your life in terms of its environment. Are the things around*
> *you helping you toward success, or are they holding you back?"*
> —W. Clement Stone

Your environment is just as important as your presentation in your quest to establish yourself and build relationships.

Once you've determined your objectives ask yourself if you're in an area that's conducive to achieving them. For example, I was born and raised in Central California, a few hours from both the Bay Area and Southern California. As much as I enjoyed my community, were it not for my career in brokerage not materializing and forcing me to relocate to a larger metro, I probably wouldn't have developed as I have—either personally or professionally.

If your goal is building and establishing business relationships, ask yourself if where you live now is the best place to do that. Even if you already live in a major city, you may be in a part that's much less conducive to your success. If you're in the middle of nowhere, you'll invariably be limited in your reach, and your surface area of luck will therefore be limited.

I always tell my clients they need to be in an area that's both inspiring and populated with successful individuals, and of course, this is typically found in wealthy enclaves. If it means stretching yourself financially and having to pick up another job, so be it. Because living in an affluent area will eventually pay for itself, especially when you encounter lucrative opportunities because of the ecosystem you're surrounded by. Moreover, you'll absorb the habits, mannerisms, and mindset that permeate the people around you. It's human nature. Conversely, if you grow up in a desolate area that's down and out, it's significantly more challenging to learn and grow.

That said, humans are incredibly robust creatures, and we often don't realize how capable we are at tackling challenges. As Tony Robbins always says, *"raise your standards,"* and by placing yourself in an environment where you're surrounded by success, you'll begin to be influenced by it and be conditioned by your environment. You will adapt.

Another way to connect with the movers and shakers of society is to position yourself in places where you can interact one on one with successful people. This could be a volunteer opportunity or a job, and it doesn't mean you need to be their colleague or have initials after your name. Roles such as even being a gate guard for a wealthy neighborhood, a teller at a bank, or a waiter at a country club can lead to interactions and therefore opportunities that may otherwise not exist. Once you're in such a position, all that's left is to take advantage of these circumstances when they arise.

Tip: Be sure to have meals with co-workers, clients or customers. This is especially important for those in business or sales roles. You may even consider creating your own co-work group that meets at the top establishments in your area. Ideally, establishments your target clients frequent. This allows you to be seen by others and gives you a way to bond with your colleagues and/or clients.

CHAPTER 3

WORDS, TONE & BODY LANGUAGE

"Words can inspire, and words can destroy. Choose yours well."
—Robin Sharma

Now that we've explored some of the fundamentals, the natural next step is for us to dive into the words we employ, including our tone and our use of body language.

You've probably been told before that our words are very powerful. But it's not just the words we say to others; it's also the internal dialogue we have with ourselves.

True mastery involves having a **grasp** of the emotions and connotations associated with them, i.e., the words and the impact they have on both you and the other party.

Learn to be a great wordsmith, and tailor your conversations to elicit the desired emotions in the people you're talking with each day. I had to learn this quickly when I left the military and was having to drink from a fire hose when I was in commercial real estate.

Cold calling, follow-ups and meetings required that I project confidence and competency, while being personable. And I quickly learned that my words, tone and body language could make or break opportunities.

I remember losing a pitch on a potential listing with the owner of an apartment complex. It was at least the second time this had happened, and I said to myself, *Okay, this can't happen again.* Nothing is a bigger motivator than failure.

That's when I enlisted the help of a coach at the time and purchased what felt like half the shelf of sales books at the local bookstore. Then I took over a week off work to immerse myself in the material. I didn't want to revist those same shortcomings again.

It also didn't help that I was beginning my career while working remotely with a team based three hours away during the middle of the COVID-19 pandemic. I know— great timing.

While my career in commercial brokerage ultimately didn't materialize, I walked away with considerable experience.

The Power of Words

There are a multitude of topics to cover as it relates to this subject and more than can fit in a single book on fostering relationships. That said, I'll share a few that I feel are of most value, and that which, if applied, will guide you on your journey with people.

Now, many experiments over the years have sought to study the power of words on human psychology. One especially powerful word, noted in the work of psychologist Ellen Langer, is the word *because.* In an experiment known as the Copy Machine Study, participants were asked to use several phrases while attempting to cut in line for the copy machine. As you might expect, of all the phrases asked by the participants, the one using the word *because* yielded the most favorable results.

Other impactful words include *yes* and *no* both of which have inherent meaning to us all at an early age. *Yes,* tends to elicit positive emotions and suggests moving forward in a desired direction. Meanwhile, *no* tends to exude the opposite effect. I suggest refraining from saying the word *no* in lieu of other words that capture your message. Whatever we can do to induce favorable thoughts and feelings in others, even if the message is less than desirable, will aid in our ability to influence and mitigate situations that could become contentious.

Remember, we're dealing with emotions when interacting with people, not so much logic. Always remember that *everyone* is directed by their feelings, albeit some more than others.

Choose Your Words Wisely

One of the best books I've read is *How to Master the Art of Selling* by Tom Hopkins. This book has practical applications to everyone's daily life and is especially pertinent for business professionals. In the book, Hopkins dives into how certain words can easily be substituted for others with better connotations, for example:

- **Agreement** or **Form** vs Contract (The word contract can carry a negative connotation.)
- **Acknowledge** or **Approve** vs Sign (People don't like signing things.)
- **Investment** vs Cost (We like to make investments in lieu of things that cost us.)
- **Provide** or **Offer** vs Sold or Sell (Sold and sell can sound too salesy.)
- **Economical** vs Cheaper (Cheaper can imply of lesser quality.)
- **Challenge** or **Hiccup** vs Problem (We want to conjure up positive emotions.)
- **Meetup** or **Get-together** vs Appointment or Meeting (Meetup or get-together are better options)

Each of these words elicit different *feelings* and conjures up different images in people's minds. That's why we only want to deploy words that evoke positive emotions, especially when we're trying to establish rapport and effectively persuade.

Take for example, the use of the word "beautiful," or "congrats"—what emotions and or images come to mind? As opposed to the words "horrible" or "terrible"? I imagine it is not the same.

For instance, if we were talking, you might notice that I refer to the social gatherings I help curate as "events," in lieu of "parties." That's because, as you can imagine, the word "party" can invoke images of people drinking excessively and acting rowdy. A mature or more sophisticated audience isn't typically going to have a desire to do that.

Tie-Downs

The following are a handful of techniques that, if employed correctly, can help build what some experts have referred to as "yes momentum." The purpose of these tie-downs is to elicit a *yes* response that helps reaffirm your message.

- *Wouldn't you agree?*
- *See where I'm coming from?*
- *Right?*
- *Sound good?*

- *Doesn't this seem like the next step?*

It also helps to occasionally mention the person's name to reengage their attention; people tend to perk up when hearing their own name. After all, people love the sound of their name, and anytime you say someone's name—followed by whatever it is you wish to convey—you help increase their retention of the information.

Open and Closed-Ended Questions

Questions that start with *who, what, when, where, why* or *how* are all much better at promoting dialogue than yes-or-no questions because they require more than a yes or no response. That said, close-ended questions do have their place, especially when you are seeking a concise answer that doesn't leave room for continued dialogue.

Saving Face

One of the keys to effectively influencing others is to avoid the rabbit hole of contentious interactions.

The socially astute individual will recognize that not everyone should get a one-size-fits-all approach to feedback, and that the delivery of a message must be tailored to the recipient, with respect to their culture and background. This can be accomplished in several ways; one approach, as we specified earlier, is to avoid words that may be counterproductive. For example, if someone did something wrong, instead of saying, *"You did XYZ,"* you could preface it with a phrase like:

- It seems
- It appears
- My understanding is

Saying, *"You're XYZ"* or *"You're doing XYZ"* or *"You've done XYZ,"* can be interpreted as if without a doubt they're in the wrong; instead, we want to bring to light something that appears to be the case but has yet to be confirmed; in other words, you're giving them room to clarify their side of the story.

Tone

While we must always be mindful of our word choice and delivery, the same is true of our tone. This is especially crucial in emails and text messages. It's very easy for things to be misinterpreted, unless enough context is given. Always err on the side of caution and refrain from anything that could be misconstrued when communicating in writing. Consider a voice or video message instead and always speak from your diaphragm.

Body Language

The better we are at reading the nonverbal cues of others, the better we can discern what states of mind people are in—whether they're hostile, nervous or receptive to us. There have been several books and videos made on the subject, and if you aren't familiar with the following language cues then I suggest you do, as it's said that about 70% of communication is nonverbal.

Anxious – signs can include eye twitching/blinking, fidgeting, crossed arms and/or legs. Additional clues can include someone vocalizing about being in pain, this can be in the from of backpain or a migraine, etc.

Receptive – People's feet tend to point in the direction they want to go—whether that's towards a particular person they wish to engage with, or towards the exit.

Unreceptive – Crossed arms and or feet (although it could be that they're simply cold as well).

Due Diligence

"People don't do what you expect but what you inspect." — Louis V. Gerstner, Jr.

Before diving headfirst into establishing a relationship, especially business or romantic in nature, be sure to ask the right questions up front. Any business veteran will understand the importance of this. I've personally spent countless time, money and energy on opportunities that, had I done my research, I would have known would lead to nowhere.

Good questions to ask include whether they genuinely need your idea, product or service and whether they are indeed the decision-maker. Thankfully, there are ways in which you can decipher this surreptitiously and tactfully, and it doesn't always involve asking them directly. Ask around, look the person up online, and when you do meet them, ask questions they'll enjoy answering to steer the conversation towards their potential want or need. We always want to ensure that expectations are set, and as the adage goes— under-promise and over-deliver.

Now that we've covered many of the fundamentals, this is where everything we've discussed comes together: when you're mentally and physically dialed in and have a solid grasp of words, tone and body language. This is what sets you apart from the masses.

CHAPTER 4

THE ART OF PERSUASION

"When dealing with people, remember you are not dealing with creatures of logic, but with creatures of emotion, creatures bristling with prejudice and motivated by pride and vanity."
—Dale Carnegie

The ability to persuade on the merits of a given course of action is the most lucrative skill set in the world, period. The individual who's gregarious, charismatic and in tune with others can wield tremendous influence.

You must learn the art of rhetoric, because we're all salespeople. Everyone is in sales, from the attorney to the president, from the teacher to the doctor and the spouse. Everyone is trying to influence someone on their idea as to why you should or shouldn't do a given thing. The sooner we realize this, and how imperative it is that we learn this skill set, the sooner we can grow our effectiveness in influencing the people in our lives.

As you engage with people, remember that people tend to value things that are earned and disregard things that are free. Position yourself favorably by incorporating this into your dialogue and, when necessary, use scarcity to create value.

Moreover, remember that familiarity breeds contempt. It becomes invariably more challenging to influence others when they lose respect. Always keep an eye on the health of your relationships with others by using a baseline of their behavior as an aid.

The best ways to learn about effective persuasion is by seeing it in-person, followed by watching videos or listening to audio books. Alternatively, you can hire a professional to help you learn this skillset. As previously stated, upon leaving the military for the private sector, I had to catch up and learn quickly. After hours spent cold calling and meeting clients in person, coupled with countless hours dedicated to reading books and receiving coaching, I began to appreciate the value in this subject.

Some of the great masters in the art of persuasion that I've learned from over the years include Tom Hopkins, Zig Ziglar, Jeffery Gitomer and Brian Tracy. I encourage you to read or listen to their books; see the appendix for titles.

Robert Cialdini distilled seven principles of influence in his book *Influence.* Here they are, along with my take on each principle.

1. **Reciprocity** – When you give something to someone, they naturally feel inclined to respond in kind. This applies whether what you've done for them is positive or negative. Humans are hard-wired to keep score.

2. **Commitment** – For example, if you're in escrow and the other party makes a deposit, even if the period of due diligence has expired, that other person is more likely to remain committed because of their investment. When you can get someone to commit, whether it's financial, their time or having them involved emotionally, they'll be much more likely to see it through.

3. **Social Proof** – A classic example of this is leveraging a well-respected individual to help you market your product or service. By capitalizing on this person's reputation, you're attaining social proof for your offering. Whether it's a potential warm introduction or something you wish to market, utilize people who are well received socially. People will begin to associate you with that person.

4. **Authority** – Those in positions of authority understandably possess greater influence over others; think the doctor over the nurse, or the president over the mayor. Leverage these people, like social proof. Seek out experts in their respective fields.

5. **Liking** – Likability is *incredibly* important. People naturally want to work alongside people who are approachable and easy to get along with. Think about how many people you've encountered over the years who were either affable or appalling—and how you engaged with them following your interaction.

6. **Scarcity** – Remember, scarcity creates value, so if you can make something be or at least appear to be a scarce resource—whether it's your time or what you have to offer—people's valuation of that resource will skyrocket. If you're not always available, you'll be seen as more valuable than someone who's always available at the drop of a hat.

7. **Unity** – People are naturally tribal and tend to gravitate towards people who are just like them. Therefore, leverage anything you have in common with those whom you wish to influence, including sports teams, politics, culture or interests.

I encourage you to find ways to incorporate these principles into your conversations, especially with clients or customers.

And according to Jordan Belfort in his book *The Way of the Wolf*, a person you seek to influence must *trust* the following:

1. **You, as an expert**
2. **Your company**
3. **Your idea, product or service**

If any of these three are lacking, you're likely to encounter hiccups. According to Belfort, objections are merely "smokescreens" for one of these three principles not being satisfied.

In keeping with the theme of this chapter, another great quote is *"He who speaks the least earns the most."* In other words, the more you talk, the more likely you are to put your foot in your mouth. Less of something can at times be best. The beauty is that the less we talk about ourselves and focus on the other person we're in conversation with, the more they'll appreciate us.

It can also be very useful to roleplay, practice and rehearse what you want to convey, so as to achieve the perfect delivery of your message. My rule of thumb is, the greater the importance, the more advanced preparation is necessary. I recall being told by a business coach to train and practice my message and responses until they became innate.

People not only want to work with people they know, like and trust; they also want to work with professionals who are sharp as a tack and have honed their craft backwards and forwards. Advertising to anyone that you're new to the industry can in some scenarios be the kiss of death. Therefore, don't go out of your way to declare that you're new to the world. That said, in some cases being the rookie, or young blood, can be advantageous, as some individuals will have a fondness for someone starting out and will want to see you succeed. A classic example of this is the young kid starting out and the older patron who is reminded of their journey when they were first getting started.

Also, if you're hoping to get in front of somebody and perhaps it's been a challenge or you have a meetup planned, refrain from giving all the information they want, at least up front. Give them a taste, or just enough to whet their appetite so they have a reason to engage with you.

This can also be achieved by leaving a video or voice message. A concise yet mysterious message—as opposed to dropping all the information up front—piques their curiosity and makes it more likely that you'll get a response back. It's also significantly more engaging when another person is able to look into your eyes and feel your personality via a video message in lieu of text.

Whoever is asking the questions is the one in control of the conversation, so take charge and ask thought-provoking questions. By starting off any interaction with topics that are of interest to that person, followed by segueing into the purpose of the interaction. This will help grab their attention and open them up to influence.

Persuasion Techniques

While this is not an in-depth exploration into the art of influence, I want to share with you at least the basics and encourage you to explore these powerful topics in greater depth. Tom Hopkins' book *How to Master the Art of Selling* is one of the best books I've read on this subject.

Persuasive techniques include assumptive language, pain points, the use of humor and emotions, objections, negotiating, alternative choice, responding to questions with questions and closes.

Assumptive Language

It should go without saying that when we're confident about our position on a matter, we exude greater influence. Therefore, it's vital to not only believe in the idea,product, or service that you're offering—but to deliver your message with absolute certainty in such a way that inspires the other person to take action.

Here's a small sample of the many assumptive language techniques you can use:

- *When you have _____, I know you'll enjoy it.*
- *I've felt the same way before; what's the best delivery address for you?*
- *This is the product I recommend; what's better, cash or card?*

- *I believe you would agree this is the best course of action.*

The key is understanding this technique and tailoring it to your own idea, product or service. It's helpful to have a wide variety of these assumptive responses at your disposal so you can avoid appearing redundant.

Pain Points

These are challenges that people have, such as the landlord with a troubling tenant, the business owner with a logistics dilemma, or the product that keeps faltering. Your job is to leverage these "pain points" to capitalize on the solution you're offering. When people are in an emotional state, that's when they take action. The key is to help walk them through their obstacles and guide them to the solution.

When I was still in commercial real estate, my mentor at the time told me, *"Christian, find their pain points."* You want to identify whatever it is that's causing them distress and resolve it. For example, as a broker, I may discover that the tenants are driving the owner insane or that the owner has been dealing with an increase in crime, which has drained him of his time and resources. When someone is unpacking something that's been heavily weighing on them, this is the time to ethically persuade them towards the solution. As Tony Robbins puts it, *"People will do more to avoid pain than they will do to gain pleasure."*

Humor

Use this when appropriate to bond with people. Having some good jokes on hand or memes to share can go a long way. For those of you not familiar with what a meme is, it's best described as an image with text—bringing to light something that's humorous in nature. The beauty of humor is that it not only adds value to people's day, by helping to lighten the mood, but it's also therapeutic and contagious. If you don't have a sense of humor, find one! Everyone has their own style, even if it's dry or self-deprecating in nature. Humor is especially effective if you're in an environment where people could benefit from a good laugh.

Emotions

Remember, people are most likely to make a decision when they're in an emotional state. Your job is to guide them, like a shepherd guiding his sheep to where he wants them to go. To paraphrase the late Zig Ziglar, people *buy* an idea, product or service through emotion, then *justify* their purchase through logic.

Objections

One of the best commercial real estate brokers I've ever met told me, "*Christian, to overcome objections, always agree.*" Of course, what is being conveyed here is to acknowledge and find something to agree with them on. You may not completely agree with the other person's objections; they may even be dead wrong. However, by agreeing with them in some capacity—even if it seems trite—will serve you much more than disagreeing. People like people who agree with them and saying anything that's remotely associated with "*I disagree,*" or worse, "*You're wrong,*" can be the kiss of death.

Remember: you will never win someone to your side, especially if you're in a heated argument, if you disagree with them by telling them they're wrong. Refraining from words that target them, like "*you,*" can help avoid catastrophe.

You win by finding areas you agree on, and you win people over by finding areas of common ground and employing the techniques referenced earlier in this book.

Arguing with the other party—especially in politics—may be good for TV ratings but it does not help engender things like cooperation. Debating only serves to drive a wedge between what one person wants and what the other person thinks.

In every situation, look for something to agree with the other party on. Make it clear that you're on their side and seeking their best interests. Doing this will make them feel heard and appreciated. There's nothing worse than when someone doesn't feel understood in a conversation, especially one that is quite meaningful to them. When you show that you're genuinely trying to understand them and can even empathize with them, you'll win major points with them.

To illustrate, two leaders may have differing views on how to achieve a given goal for their constituents. If the opposing parties were to find commonalities on which to agree, even if it's something as trivial as a shared desire to improve a given area of the government, this will always be more productive than seeking to out-maneuver the other in verbal judo.

Unfortunately, the media loves to add fuel to the fire and create division in our society. They don't want us working together. They want us divided.

Negotiating

Of all the interpersonal skills, this is one of the most important and potentially lucrative. We all negotiate multiple times every day in both our work and personal lives, whether we're aware of it or not. We negotiate with our business partners, clients and customers and with our spouses, friends and the strangers we meet. Unfortunately, the average person receives almost zero training in negotiations, perhaps except for those in business. Business expert Chris Croft has articulated the following 12 'commandments':

1. If you don't ask, you don't get.
2. Realize that you're never going to lose the deal, because you can always crumble.
3. Instead of saying no, offer to trade.
4. View the process as a game: be detached and learn.
5. Aim for a win/win, by questioning and then trading.
6. Set your 'walk away' point, and NEVER go beyond it.
7. Prepare and then probe for their possible weaknesses, in order to feel stronger.
8. Try to avoid opening first.
9. Opening offers: open wide, and not with a round number.
10. Move in small steps.
11. Move by trading: "If you... then I..."
12. Watch out for the nibble, and don't allow it.

I also suggest incorporating the following:

- Strive to remain stoic, which will make it more difficult for the other party to read you.
- Consider not answering calls from unknown numbers, as a call could catch you off guard and potentially lead to poor negotiating on your end. For those who don't have this luxury and must accept calls, be mindful.

Alternative Choice

People naturally want to feel in control, and they love being able to choose between various options. The alternative choice technique seeks to satisfy this innate human desire by providing options to the recipient.

Examples include:

- *How's Thursday or Friday?*
- *What time works best, 2 or 3 p.m.?*
- *What day works best for delivery—the 1st or the 2nd?*

As you can see, this can be used in a multitude of different ways, and yet each response leads the other person towards the desired objective.

Question with a Question

Another useful technique is to respond to a question with a question. Perhaps you simply need to understand the question better, or maybe you want to buy yourself enough time to figure out the answer. Asking a question back, when done appropriately and tactfully, can enhance your understanding.

Examples include:

- **Prospect:** What kind of property do you have available?
  You: Are you looking for an apartment complex or industrial property?

- **Prospect:** Do you have any vehicles for sale?
  You: Are you looking for a sedan or coupe?

- **Prospect:** What's your take on _____?
  You: Are you referring to X, Y, or Z?

Remember to always set expectations, and it's better to over-communicate than under-communicate.

Closes

The close, also known as going for "the order" or "ask," is the last step in the process of persuading someone on an idea, product or service. We always want to ensure that we're taking this step with the decision-maker, while remaining seated the entire time and staying positive—regardless of the outcome. And, while there are a plethora of closing techniques out there, the key is that after you go for the "close," you keep quiet and wait until they respond. Doing otherwise will only undermine your ability to persuade them. If need be—and if things start to get awkward after waiting a minute or two—then you may consider smiling or employing some other type of device to elicit a response, but don't say anything.

Humor can also be a great way to complement your close, as it helps to relieve pressure. Remember, we want people to feel comfortable and relaxed, not tense and uptight about any commitment.

The following are several closing techniques that I've absorbed from experts such as Tom Hopkins, Brian Tracy, Grant Cardone and Zig Ziglar (tailor them as you see fit):

Ben Franklin Close

This is essentially a pro and con list made between you and the other party. The aim of this approach is to guide the other party towards highlighting what they have to gain from their investment. When this is done right, you help them rationalize the reason to move forward by demonstrating that the pros outweigh the cons.

You: Why don't we weigh the pros and cons? –or– What's something to be gained?
Prospect: *XYZ*
You: What's a potential negative?
Prospect: *XYZ*

And you go back and forth between the two.

Reduce to the Penny Close

This closing technique is intended to highlight the trivial nature of the investment the other person is making. For example, they may be investing $7,000 for a year's worth of service; however, when broken down on an hourly basis the investment is only 80 cents per hour.

By acknowledging the hourly investment of 80 cents, as opposed to the $7,000 per year, you help juxtapose the value they are receiving, in a way that's logical and highlighting the minimal investment required of them. If this can also be delivered with a sense of humor, this is an added bonus when done tactfully.

Agreement Close

This approach involves you simply agreeing with the other party when faced with an objection, followed by both vocalizing and indicating to them next steps. Here's an example:

Prospect: *It's a lot of money*
You: *I agree, it's a sizable investment. Now you just need to initial/approve here and here.*

Think About It Close

When you encounter the classic "Let me think about it" response from a prospect, consider employing this tactic.

Prospect: *I still need to give it some thought.*
You: *I hear ya; that said, if I might ask, is it _____, _____, or _____?*

This helps to vet out the objections they have and makes us aware of them so we can overcome these obstacles. Think of *price*, *terms* or *product/service* as potential fill-in-the-blanks.

Sharp Angle Close

In this technique, you respond to an ask by the other party by hypothetically agreeing, then asking them to approve the agreement.

Prospect: *Can I have an extra _____ in addition to the _____?*
You: *If I offer that, would you move forward with our agreement?*

Rule Out Close

Use this when you're seeking to rule out any other possible excuses that may arise, so as to prevent any future surprises.

Prospect: *Thanks for sharing info on _____.*
You: *Happy to; would there be any reason why we can't move forward?*

Wet-Signature Close

When it's time for the other party to make a commitment to your product or service, hold the pen out in front of you and wait for them to grab it—even if you need to hold the pen for an uncomfortable length of time. They will naturally feel compelled to grab the pen from you.

This can also be achieved with a handshake; simply extend your hand, after going for the close, and leave it extended until they grab and shake it. Remember, after you've reached your hand out, do not say one thing until they've agreed.

These are some techniques you can employ to achieve your objective.

Always go for the ask, and remember, closed mouths don't get fed.

Meeting in Person

Echoing back earlier in the book, be sure to ask yourself, "What is the purpose for the two of us getting together?" For those in business or dating, ask yourself, "Have I successfully qualified this person?" We want to always be sure that they satisfy our parameters and that there's mutual interest. The last thing you want is to connect with someone who may not be that interested in the first place. Remember, protect your time and resources.

Any time you can, and it makes sense, you want to meet people in person, especially when you have something important to discuss or when you're meeting them for the first time. The phone is for setting up a time to get together, whether it's a client or a date. Unless you look like Quasimodo or the Crypt-Keeper, keep the phone conversation short and save what you want to discuss for when you meet in person. Why, you may ask? Because connecting in person will significantly enhance your ability to persuade.

Tip: When shaking someone's hand, be sure to stand up, if possible, look the other person in the eye, and give a firm handshake. It may seem common sense, but I still encounter people that can't do this to save their life.

Breaking Bread

One of the best ways to meet others and nurture relationships is over meals—it's something humans have done for millennia. The same can be said of sharing a spirituous drink with somebody. Again, while you should be mindful of where you allocate your resources, be sure to dedicate a portion of your budget to dining and socializing with others. I guarantee it will pay dividends when done smartly.

For those who aren't in business and have no desire to be, there's still much value in investing in meals. I find it amusing whenever I hear someone espouse cutting back on certain items, such as grabbing that cup of coffee in the morning, for fear it will rob you of your savings. My response to this is unequivocally "Yes." You *will* be robbing yourself of money—millions of dollars, to be exact—in business that you would have otherwise made had you enjoyed that cup of coffee and socialized with fellow patrons. Not to mention the social capital you would have accrued over the years meeting people at various coffee shops. The same goes for going out to eat with prospects or clients.

So yes, there is a cost. If someone is in the mentality of being stingy with money or is afraid of spending too much on items such as coffee or lunch, then they are inviting a mindset that's not of abundance but that of scarcity. Remember the adage, *"The more you give, the more you receive."* It takes money to make money.

I've even seen people hoard their friends like money, not wanting others to interact with their friends unless they're involved in some way. Now, unless this other person is a client or significant other, hoarding contacts exudes scarcity.

When you come from a position of abundance, again within reason, you attract more of it into your life. On the other hand, people who penny-pinch over everything are inviting more of that into their existence. Even though some resources are inherently finite, there is plenty of opportunities to produce wealth and build valuable relationships.

Tip: If you're meeting with someone outside, try to avoid wearing sunglasses, when possible, as it can diminish the ability to connect with the other person on a deeper level.

Wearing sunglasses doesn't allow for the eyes to be viewed, which is critical when building trust.

Restaurants

As someone I know from the U.K. once put it, America has a great bar scene. And I would have to agree with him. High-end establishments such as restaurants, bars, resorts and lounges can be great places to meet people. You don't need to touch any alcohol; a non-alcoholic beverage or meal will suffice. Now, my suggestion is to identify the hot spot for your target audience and go there each day.

Over time, not only will you meet many people (as long as you make the effort), you'll also get to know the entire staff. And guess what? Those staff and patrons know other people, and will invariably introduce you to those people, especially if they like you. You may even consider tipping higher than you normally do for specific people—you'll find that they'll be more inclined to take care of you, whether that's with drinks or introducing you to people of value.

Moreover, once you've become a regular, staff will begin to acknowledge you when you walk in, giving you an almost celebrity-like aura. This will invariably attract attention from other guests, prompting people to reach out and interact with you as if you were a magnet. Now imagine going to such a place with your prospects, friends or a date, and how much more attractive this reception will make you.

After you've done this for a period, consider pivoting to another location and replicating the same process. Now obviously, your food bill will be going up significantly each month, but so will your social capital. And, if you implement this strategically, you'll begin to see the fruits of your labor. As you continue to make going out a part of your daily ritual, you'll eventually get to know who the movers and shakers are and amass a (figurative) Rolodex. All your work will begin to compound, and the next step will be leveraging these relationships. Once again, these can be personal or business relationships.

Interpersonal Skills

After vetting the other person out and when finally getting together with the other person, you'll want to open the dialogue with how they're doing both personally and professionally. Ensure you give enough time and show genuine interest before segueing into business. Ask questions you know they'll enjoy answering. This serves three purposes. First, it will grab their attention. Second, people enjoy talking about themselves. And third, they'll feel the desire to reciprocate, giving you the opportunity to talk.

After engaging in personal talk, you can transition into exploring business or whatever the purpose of the get-together is. Now, as I converse with people, I try to always check their pulse as it relates to their time schedule. There's nothing like being stuck in a conversation with a chatty Kathy when you have somewhere to be. One thing you can do so as to avoid being stuck in conversation too long is to set a timer on your phone. Depending on the person and nature of the meetup, I may set up a few muted alarms. This helps me to remain totally focused without being distracted about the time and other plans I may have that day. The muted alarm is also less disruptive to those around you.

The saying *"Scarcity creates value"* holds true both in personal and business relationships. Always being available can potentially convey lesser value to a business or romantic interest. We want to show that we're both chasing excellence and in keeping with our mission and purpose in life. Position yourself as a scarce resource, and people will respond accordingly.

Tip: People tend to remember the first and the last of any given thing, be it a meeting, interview, or event, while everything in between tends to lack the same degree of retainment. For this reason, it's best if you're the first person to go for something or the last.

When you meet with someone—particularly a client or prospective one—strive to always give them something.

Why? Two reasons. First, people are reciprocal in nature, and they'll have an instinctive desire to do something for you in return. Second, when you hand them something, even if it's a piece of paper with info on it, they're likely to have it in their presence. Be that in their car, house or office. And guess what? Every time they see it, they'll be reminded of you. This isn't possible if you only send them information digitally, which can be easily lost in the barrage of messages they may receive.

Remember to focus on what matters the most to the person you're speaking with. As much as we may want to share our lives with others, people would rather have the focus of the conversation on themselves.

In general, you want the other person doing most of the talking, with you asking the questions. And remember to listen, because you'll invariably be quizzed to demonstrate your attentiveness in time. Your job is to ask questions and listen.

Always strive to find common ground with people, as this is an instant rapport builder. For example, you may have attended the same university, share the same hobby, or love the same sports team.

Tip: An easy way to remember someone's name is to say their name three times in your head or associate their name with something—the more outlandish the better. For instance, if someone is named Johnny, think 'Johnny Appleseed.' Another is to say their name throughout the conversation. When you first meet someone, you might say, "Great to meet you, Bob," and then work Bob's name into several other sentences as appropriate.

To echo Harvey Mackay's book, *Dig Your Well Before You're Thirsty,* we need to plant the seeds before we can enjoy the fruits of our labor—with relationships as with anything in life.

Give service to others as often and as early as possible (within reason, of course—you still need to protect your time and energy) and always give value first.

I firmly believe that social capital is the most lucrative form of currency in the world.

It has allowed many world figures to attain success, be it galvanizing support for a noble cause or repelling an invasion. While monetary capital is vital, social capital can be what allows for one business to succeed over another who may have equal financial strength. Those who are in the media are in a particular advantage because of the familiarity they have with their audience, of which can be channeled towards business ventures or political objectives.

Everyone you meet, from the average Joe walking down the street to the garbage collector, and of course your local business magnates, possess power and influence in varying degrees.

Therefore, be mindful of everyone you engage with; never underestimate their power or who they may know. Receive everyone cordially and with due respect. I've both observed and have been the recipient of comments that would create ill will, with the other person not being fully aware of who they're addressing. One time I went to a Christmas party where one of the hosts, while attempting to address a matter, was disrespected by an inebriated guest—only for that guest to find out shortly after that the person they slighted was one of the hosts. They were then promptly asked to leave and never return.

One of the quotes that stands out to me from Robert Greene's book, *The 48 Laws of Power*, is "Know Who You're Dealing With—Do Not Offend The Wrong Person."

People of course tend to respond in kind to each other—whether it's positive or negative.

The relationship expert and author Corey Wayne used a particularly good analogy: a healthy relationship is like playing tennis. It's symbiotic in that both players are hitting the ball back and forth across the court; in essence, meeting each other's needs. However, if things begin to deviate and you're having to run to the other side of the court to hit the ball back, it might be time to re-evaluate the relationship.

In that case, start by determining whether this one-sidedness is even intentional on their part. If it is indeed the case that they have lost interest, perhaps you may need to enhance the perceived value you offer, which is clearly not being appreciated by the other person.

"Whatever you tolerate, you invite more of into your life."
—Corey Wayne

If someone chooses not to respond to your calls or messages and it becomes clear that it's intentional, you must give them the gift of withdrawing yourself.

CHAPTER 5

ENGAGING UNCONVENTIONALLY

"IQ operates the world, EQ runs it."
—Habib Bakshi

Growing up, and even to this day, I've been fascinated by military history, especially the tactics and strategies military leaders have employed to achieve success. This, coupled with generations of ancestors who have served since before the U.S. even existed, inspired me to pursue a career in the military. After college, I joined the Navy with my sights set on special operations. I remember reading and studying a great deal about those who have served in the special warfare community and their mentality. What stood out to me most, in addition to their incredible mental tenacity, was how they operated in an unorthodox manner. This awareness was further compounded when I began the special ops pipeline. Ultimately, while I didn't succeed in this career path, I learned a great deal in the process. I attribute some of the success I've experienced to my exposure to the special operations community. Among the many things I learned, thinking unconventionally was one of the great takeaways.

Personal story: When I realized I needed a change in direction career wise, after careful thought, I made the decision to relocate to Southern California to further my career. Of course, most people trying to get a job go online and submit their resume—which, to be fair, is what most companies ask candidates to do.

Given my background and the nature of the finance industry, I recognized that my resume wouldn't be as competitive if I were to just send it via traditional channels, i.e., uploading and sending it to hiring managers. Therefore, I decided the best option would be for me to drive four hours down to Newport Beach, with about 20 resumes, and simply knock on doors. And that's exactly what I did; I put on a blazer and walked into the various commercial real estate firms in town, from the main brokerage houses to family offices, to private equity firms.

People were surprised to have someone drive four hours from home without anything lined up and inquire at the front desk if they were hiring. The reason? No one does it. Employers want you to submit your resume via email and leave the selection process to an individual who knows nothing of you or your potential worth.

It's a robotic process, in which thousands of applicants apply hoping to receive their "golden ticket."

As you might expect, I was offered a few opportunities. Now, these opportunities weren't exactly what I wanted, so I decided to hold off until I found something that was a better fit for me. As the saying goes, the fortune is in the follow-up. And so, I followed up with a gentleman who happened to be a veteran, whom I'd met earlier when I was visiting various companies. He then offered me an opportunity that fit my criteria. Remember, be sure to find common ground with anybody you meet, whether it's a college alumnus, someone from the same hometown, a similar language, religion, politics, sports team, or anything else that bonds you.

We live in one of the most competitive times in history. In the past, you competed with people in your community or region for resources. Now you're competing with people across the country and the world, thanks to advances in technology and the work-from-home revolution. Additionally, with the rise of AI and other progress in tech, fewer and fewer people will be needed to complete jobs.

I say all of this as further evidence that you must continue to approach your life, and each of your objectives in life, unconventionally.

I once had a retail broker tell me to try and take a different path each time I traveled to the same place (like work) to avoid getting stuck in a routine. In case you're wondering, the reason is because you'll begin to notice different things on your drive—and it allows you to explore different ideas and see more aspects of what's going on in your city.

It's because of this same principle that even what may seem to be a misfortune can bring about success or a new way of looking at things. To illustrate, one time I misplaced my car keys for almost a week, and I was dependent on various drivers to get around. However, this forced me to meet various people who were chauffeuring me around. The disruption to my routine forced me to interact in different ways and do things differently.

If you're concerned about reaching out or deviating from the norm due to a fear of rejection, remember that most people really don't care about you. They're more interested in themselves. People also tend to forget things. As the adage goes, time heals all wounds. Unless medical technology improves quite a bit, the vast majority of people alive today will be forgotten about over time. Future generations will be too absorbed in their own affairs to even consider what someone said or did today that was offbeat.

I try to always underscore the importance of trying to stand apart from everyone else. Society and the media have done a great job of grooming everyone to march lockstep towards the prevailing narrative. This typically involves going to school, receiving good grades, striving to attend a top university, landing a high-paying job... and you get the picture. It's like a conveyor belt.

In a world with around 7 billion people, how are you standing out from the masses? What makes you unique and special? How do you delineate yourself from the competition, especially if you're in the world of finance where you're competing with very well-connected individuals who may have pedigree on their side.

Hint: Go against the grain.

There are a multitude of ways to accomplish this, from reaching out to people uniquely to positioning yourself astutely. Now, depending on the person we wish to get a hold of, we may have to exercise a greater degree of finesse, especially the more prominent a person is socially.

Remember, if you really want something to materialize, keep working at it—and try approaching it from different angles. You may have even thought that you've exhausted all options, only to discover one that works. Therein lies the value of consulting with others and seeking answers from different sources.

Personal story: There's a celebrity I'm acquainted with (we'll call him John) whom I'd been trying to get a hold of for collaboration. However, it had always been a challenge to get him on the phone. I'd send text messages, only to have my messages fall on deaf ears, as he always had his phone set to voice message. Now, I could have written it off—after sending message after message via text. However, I finally thought, why not take a different approach? I instead opted to send a voice message instead. Now some of you may say that's not unique, and I agree. However, most people don't use it. And the fourth time I sent a message, I received a call from John. Video messages are even better. There's nothing like looking into another person's eyes and reading their vibe. If you can't meet in person or talk over the phone, sending a video message is the next best way to capture someone's attention.

Strategy

Be strategic about where you spend your time. The following are among the best places to meet the most people in the shortest amount of time:

- **Gym** – Alternate, if possible, between morning and afternoons to ensure you meet different people.
- **Breakfast** – Go to the top destinations that people you wish to connect with gravitate towards.
- **Lunch** – Same thing; top lunch spots. (Sit at the bar.)
- **Dinner** – Top dinner spots are typically high-end establishments—if this is the audience you're targeting. (Sit at the bar.)
- **Walking the Dog** – Pets are a great excuse to interact with people, because they force you to walk around, and you'll invariably run into and meet new people. Even if you don't have a dog, go for walks around your home and workplace. You'll undoubtedly meet

people on your stroll who will introduce you to their people.

Come up with a similar strategy for weekends as well, which could include attending religious services or other regular social functions. Doing this will increase your surface area of luck. This is especially pertinent to those of you whose product or service could be provided to anyone, i.e., realtors, mortgage professionals, etc.

Alternative Gifts

Gift-giving has been a hallmark of relationships for millennia, serving as a gesture of solidarity. There are many ways in which you can incorporate this practice into your interactions with others, whether it be for a celebratory occasion, gesture of appreciation or even a career opportunity. I have heard of encounters where someone seeking a specific role at a company sent a shoe to their prospective employer as a means to 'get their foot in the door.' But it doesn't have to be a shoe; you could also send a piece of sports memorabilia, or perhaps an item or gift card that demonstrates that you've done your homework for that specific individual or group. You can find clues on what will connect with them via their website bios or LinkedIn. Exercising good judgment is highly advised, so as to not appear too invasive or even desperate. However, these tactics, when executed appropriately, can be great ways to grab somebody's attention.

Tip: You may need to be discreet at times when it comes to your gift-giving, particularly if others might expect to receive one as well. I recall reading an experience from a fellow author who was the client of a financial services professional. After visiting the office one day and observing cases of wine, he later happened to run into the secretary out in town and casually inquired about the wine. Not knowing that he hadn't been given one, she mentioned that those bottles of wine were reserved for her boss's special clients. When he heard this, he decided to cease using his financial advisor. An example of this can be best illustrated with birthday invitations.

Social Proof

Social proof is one of the most powerful levers you can pull to capture an audience. After all, what compels us to engage with somebody we've never met is often their association with other people we know. Because we often don't have the time, nor particularly the desire to vet everyone we meet, we must often rely on visual and auditory cues, to include social proof from others, to assess people. When you're establishing yourself, whether in a new company or town or with a friend or romantic interest, it's critical to have others serve as testament to your character and reputation.

Social Proof & Social Media

One effective strategy for establishing social proof, especially when trying to connect with a person of influence on social media is to first engage and befriend/follow their friends and associates. By engaging with these people and their content first you help to ensure that your "target person" will engage with you. Moreover, as you gain followers from their network and showcase your personality, you enhance the likelihood of them reciprocating by following you back and engaging with your own content.

Now, depending on how quickly you wish to engage with them, you may consider sending them a video message in lieu of the standard direct message via text. Remember, you need to find ways to stand out from the hundreds or even thousands of messages they receive each day.

Tip: A great way to build goodwill with those you follow on social media, and it doesn't require much effort is sharing people's stories or posts, especially if they're trying to spread the word about something. Moreover, they are likely to respond in kind when you have something you may wish to share to the world. Additionally, liking and commenting on their content will also pay dividends.

Curating Your Social Media Presence

One of the many benefits of social media includes the opportunity to build your personal brand and foster familiarity with a potentially large audience. As seen in viral content which can provide immense reach. Depending on the platform, you can do this by sharing your activity via posts, reels, or stories. It works best when we share our lives authentically with others and give people a reason to reach out, whether that's asking a question or conducting a survey to your audience.

Remember, we live in an attention economy, and attention spans are getting shorter. The more you can occupy the real estate in people's minds as they go about their daily lives, the likelier it is that they'll engage with you. You will also increase your surface area of luck when people begin recalling you in conversation with others and encounter scenarios in their daily life that may be germane to you and what you do. These reasons could be career and investment opportunities, an invite to that private event or country club, or romantic interest.

Tip: People will develop a stronger bond with you the more you relate to them. Those who give off a near-perfect image on social platforms run the risk of deviating from the humanity that's often required to truly bond with another person, not to mention triggering envy. On the other hand, the one who opens up to their audience (within reason, of course) has the opportunity to connect on a deeper level. Law number 46 from Robert Greene's book, The 48 Laws of Power, is titled "Never Appear Too Perfect."

If you're not on or active on social media, as in your personal account and you're in business, then you're undermining your own success. It's no longer possible (unless you're Bill Gates or Elon Musk) to sit back with little to no digital presence and rely soley on word of mouth. If you're not active on social media, it's *"Out of sight, out of mind."* Again, this is pertaining to your personal account not a business one you may have.

For example, there are times when I'm putting together a small outing with friends or helping to put together a sizable group to go yachting, and it's often the people in my social media feed who receive the invite first because they're top of mind.

Content Creation

Ask anyone who's been in the entertainment industry, and they'll share with you the change that's occurred with the rise of social media, especially reels, stories and TikTok. Creating content that has the potential to go viral can be like hitting the jackpot. Spend time researching what other content creators are doing and learn how to complement the algorithms that dictate what's shown to viewers.

Tip: Everybody loves a good laugh. If you can create content that's humorous, it's a plus. So instead of making a quick video about numbers and where the market is or something that may come across as mundane, consider a comedic spin on content that you produce.

I advise posting content as often as you can, posing questions to give your followers a reason to engage with you. Remember, we want to make it as easy as possible for people to reach out to us. Another great way to increase your visibility and add value is to create a public or private niche group on a social media platform or website.

In your content, strive to always show your face and address your audience as if you're only talking to one person. So instead of saying, "Hey guys," or "Hey everyone," try saying, "Hey," followed by your message.

Tip: Ensure that people can see your eyes as often as possible. This allows your audience and viewers to build a better rapport with you and trust. Wearing sunglasses can obstruct this ability to bond.

Handwritten Letters

Another idea I learned was from author and sales expert Tom Hopkins, who encourages his readers to send handwritten thank-you notes to people. His rationale is that the notes show you took the extra time to go through the process of writing and sending a letter—and that your presence, in the form of a card, is likely to remain within a person's sphere, continually reminding them of you.

Tip: Given the proliferation of new technology in our lives, the concept of handwritten letters has also been utilized by direct mail marketing companies, where robots create lifelike handwritten notes to people. Be sure, if you write a note, that it conveys that you actually wrote it and not some robot. These artificial hand-written letters have become more popular and are incredibly real looking.

Door Knocking

While certainly not a new approach to engaging with people, door knocking can be particularly effective when delivered astutely—especially when seeking career, partnership or client acquisition opportunities. For instance, consider going to the company you wish to work for and asking to see the hiring manager. Again, success hinges on doing the things that most people aren't willing to do.

Legitimate Reasons to Reach Out

Wishing someone a happy birthday or anniversary gives you a great touch point. Start by making it a habit to check your social media platforms, such as Facebook and LinkedIn, to see whose birthday it is today. Then be sure to save their birthday under their contact information in your phone.

Video & Voice Messages

I've touched on this earlier, consider communicating via video messages or voice messages when you're unable to speak on the phone with someone or meet in-person.

GIFs

Using animated images like GIFs can be a great way to stand out. For example, you could have an animated profile picture to make your emails stand out from the masses of other emails people receive, or you could even animate your signature block to set yourself apart. Again, be creative and delineate yourself.

Wearing Conversations

Wearing clothing that attracts attention can help spark conversations that would otherwise never happen. Try wearing logoed hats or polos such as that of a sports team, golf company, or even a lapel pin representing your business on your blazer. The same can be accomplished by wearing high-end or dressy attire that easily stands out from the crowd. The easier you make it for people to grab onto something to spark conversation, the better. This is extended to cars, backpacks, travel gear, and virtually anything that is seen in public, all of which can be a means to market yourself and spark conversation that may lead to opportunities. Conversely, comment on someone else's attire and you may soon find that you've made a new friend or client.

Social Magnet

Your goal, ultimately, is to have others gravitate towards you. You've seen this, of course, in the celebrity, prominent business professional or politician who draws people to them. Emulate what others are doing on social media and in person so that you become a magnet, as opposed to having to reach out to everyone yourself. Of course, everybody starts off being the one who must initiate contact, especially career wise. But it's like going fishing; when you have multiple poles in the water, you automatically increase your odds of catching something. Unless you're a recluse or are already where you want to be, work to be seen through as many channels as possible.

Writing

Whether it's a book, blog or article, writing can be an effective way to engage a new audience and create a dent in the universe. You don't need to write every day or create a book that's hundreds of pages; useful e-guides can be only a few pages to be effective. You also don't need to be an expert for many years to produce work that is of value.

That said, I recommend writing on a niche you excel at or are passionate about. For example, if you recently graduated from college, you could write a how-to guide to help incoming college students navigate college life and share tips you wish you had known when you were at that stage. It could even be a niche within college life, like sports or a specific major. The key is simply to write about something that you're passionate about.

In addition, you can write while on the go, by leveraging the mic on your phone or laptop. You can then revise it later when you're in front of your computer. You may even consider having someone write on your behalf if you're constrained on time.

Now, as it relates to books. There are several reasons to write a book. First, you'll be an author and seen as an authority figure on the subject. Second, you'll stand out when meeting with employers or prospective business partners. And third, it can lead to serendipitous events such as a career, relationship or other opportunity—simply because you're giving people more opportunities to encounter and engage with you.

Movers & Shakers

One of the best ways to meet people, is to find your local 'town square.' Historically, this has been the place where people congregate. Today, it's often your local shopping center. To illustrate, I live near a major shopping center in Newport Beach that essentially functions as the city's town square. Each time I walk around there or grab lunch at one of the many restaurants, I'm almost guaranteed to run into someone I know, and I'm often introduced to the people that they're with.

Your town square could be a retail center or a place of worship. Even restaurants can serve as mini town squares. Go to where the people you wish to meet are going and use these places to increase your visibility amongst the movers and shakers and the general public.

In the words of Robert Greene, court attention at all cost. This is especially relevant following the work from home environment that we live in today. If you're an introvert, then leverage a friend or colleague to engage with and befriend others. Play to your strengths.

Personal Website

I highly recommend creating a personal website that's centered around you and showcases your personal brand to the world. This can be done easily with the help of site builders like Wix or WordPress. Alternatively, you can pay someone to create one for you or leverage AI. That said, if you're like me, you'll want to be able to access your site at any time and tailor it exactly to your liking, which can be more difficult if you've outsourced your website completely to a third party.

Sidenote: Do your best to capture as many email addresses as you can. This is best accomplished via a lead magnet, which, if you're not familiar with it, is a reward you offer in exchange for someone's email. The CTA (call to action) can be a single sentence that offers this reward.

To illustrate, on your social media account you can have an emoji of a finger pointing down to a link. And next to the link is a tagline that conveys a brief yet persuasive sentence that incentivizes people to take action by clicking the link, then directs them to your website to receive their reward. This is your lead magnet.

Speaking of your email, I recommend not using your work email, unless you're a partner at your company—in case you decide to leave.

News Media

Establishing and building relationships with various news platforms, such as business journals, magazines, news-papers, and online articles can be instrumental. Particularly the editors of these companies.

Podcasts

Consider making an appearance on a popular podcast or creating your own with people of complementary backgrounds.

LinkedIn

This platform is a goldmine. If fully utilized, it can lead to incredible opportunities. One way to build relationships quickly, whether in your local area or while traveling, is to reach out to people with a similar background to you and see if they're open to meeting up over lunch or coffee. Remember, the more people you meet and help, the more you'll compound your reach. If you meet 20 new people per week for a decade, you will have met 10,400 people. These 10,400 people know hundreds if not thousands of other people who will mention you in some capacity at some point, exponentially growing your visibility. You are in essence creating disciples, especially if you help these people. For example, there are many business professionals who serve as adjunct professors to gain greater visibility while helping the next generation.

Below is a way in which you may consider sending a message to someone that you've never met before:

Joe, (Less formal)

Great post on _____. (Referencing a post they made or engaged with; note I would suggest engaging with their content as well.)

I also attended XYZ college/from the same hometown. *(Leverage common ground.)*

Would be great to connect. (I'm not being assumptive, but making it known that I'd like to interact with them.)

Christian White

777-777-7777

Be sure that your message is as personalized as you can make it and ensure that it doesn't appear to be a spam message, that so many are accustomed to receiving.

You should hear back from them soon. If, however, you don't, then wait about a week and circle back via another medium. Perhaps this time you may call or send a video message instead.

Tip: If there's a particular career you hope to have, reach out to somebody who's already doing it, either via a call or video message, and ask if they would be open to grabbing coffee or lunch. You can even send them a handwritten letter that references an interest they have, something the two of you have in common, or something that may make them chuckle.

Self-Assessment

As you seek to position yourself to maximize your relationships, try exploring your strengths and weaknesses. What do you feel you excel at compared to others and vice versa? Now take inventory of those strengths and outsource the things that you may struggle with. What's your "zone of genius"? Figure out what you possess that very few people have, and leverage this.

CHAPTER 6

THE GREAT CHALLENGE

"Courage isn't having the strength to go on—it is going on when you don't have strength."
—Napoleon Bonaparte

Whether you're a business professional or seeking to build new relationships, getting in front of people, especially a specific person, can be challenging at times. Even once you manage to do so, the next hurdle is naturally cultivating a relationship and remaining top of mind, especially if you're seeking to provide your idea, product or service.

Questions that arise include the following:

- How do I get in front of this person?
- How do I offer value that's unique and germane to them?
- How do I distinguish myself, and how can I foster an ongoing relationship with them?

Even I find myself asking these questions at times. But the thing is, if you can identify alternative means to engage, you *will* find success. Therefore, we need to have something of great value to offer, something that gives us a great reason to reach out.

Now, short of being a celebrity, one of the best ways to engage with someone is to invite them to a curated social event you've helped put together. By offering an atypical experience and seeking to satisfy as many areas of potential interest to them. The topic of hosting social affairs will be expanded upon later in the book.

One strategy you can employ to engage with someone, especially if they've been a challenge to get ahold of is by identifying the people that they are either friends with or who they associate with in business. Depending on where you are as it relates to this process, the plan is to interact with and serve as a resource to these people. Therefore, you will get closer and closer to the person you are ultimately wanting to engage with. As you may have observed, this is not necessarily a quick approach to engaging with your target person but one that may require time. Use this technique if you are unable to communicate with your target. The way in which you can accomplish all of this is by leveraging social platforms, such as LinkedIn or Instagram and other mediums such as email or reaching out through other means.

One way to brainstorm prospective prospects is to begin by identifying the top 10 individuals that you wish to engage with. Naturally, the more prominent of a person you are wishing to interact with, the more potential hurdles there may be.

Investing in Relationships

While I don't advocate being cavalier with your finances, I do believe that one of the best investments you can make is in the people in your life from family, friends, colleagues and clients. I've seen the compounding benefits of this firsthand.

Give & Take

There's a passage in the Bible that says, "It is more blessed to give than to receive" (Acts 20:35). There's nothing like helping a fellow human being, and it can be as simple as giving someone a ride, listening to them with your undivided attention, or covering their meal. Remember what I mentioned earlier regarding our actions and how they affect the way people feel? Well, even the simple things we do, and gestures is appreciated by others and observed, whether we're fully aware of it or not. Moreover, the good deeds we do, especially when there's no strings attached tends to come back to us tenfold.

Giving value to someone else can also be as simple as making the other person laugh or sending them a meme. Why comedy? Because everyone loves a good laugh, it's contagious, and they will associate positive feelings with you. Moreover, they may share your joke or meme with a friend, who may very well share it with another, with word circling back identifying you as the source. For instance, my friend Pouya Hashemi, a comedian and influencer, leverages his sense of humor to connect with people both via social media and in person. Pouya produces short-form video content that makes light of what's happening in today's pop culture.

Tip: You can also hit two birds with one stone by creating a group chat or email thread with friends or clients, not only to stay in touch with them, but also to keep them entertained and add value to their day.

Many of these ways to be resourceful require little investment aside from a few minutes of your time. Even a genuine compliment can go a long way. Studies have shown that servers who compliment their guests tend to get bigger tips, and the mere act of acknowledging someone can work wonders. Leverage simple things you can offer, even asking people how their day is going or how you can help them. As long as it's from the heart, it's guaranteed to be worth your time.

I once asked a prominent businessman for advice, and his best piece of advice was to be likable. This stood out to me because it wasn't what I expected to hear. That said, he considered this a key factor in his success. Likability is huge; I've seen many people, whether they were competent or otherwise, excel simply because they were well received.

While in the Navy, I was in training with a man I'll call Bob. Who was always forgetting things and not paying attention. However, he had a great sense of humor and would often crack jokes and act in jaw-dropping ways, much to the amusement of everyone in the class and instructors. So, while he did get the class in trouble from time to time, he was still well received—largely because he provided value in the form of comedic entertainment to the class. Humor went a long way to lighten everyone's mood.

It's an interesting world we live in. One would think that someone needs to do a conventionally "good job" to succeed, and conduct themselves like everyone else, when in fact there are quite a few people out there who, for one reason or another, are in their positions because of likability, cronyism, or being resourceful in some capacity.

Now, as it relates to money and investing in relationships, it never ceases to amaze me how many people allow money to infringe on their ability to foster relationships. We must invest in people and activities that will enable us to prosper, whether this means spending money on meals, taking trips, golfing or skiing.

Now, you need not invest in activities that require extensive use of funds. What's important is that you stay true to yourself and come from a place of sincerity. People, especially those who are successful, can typically decipher if you're being genuine. And, regarding how to connect with people of clout and wealth, it's about being a *standout* resource. For example, say you just met a successful real estate developer at the local lunch spot, and the following day, you run into an investor who's seeking a buyer for a commercial property. By helping the two of them connect, you accomplish three things. First, both will appreciate the introduction and feel inclined to reciprocate, whether or not the introduction you made leads to business. Second, the two of them may even become friends. Third, there may be someone else in their network who could be of value to either one.

Introducing people who are complementary to one another will compound over time into both personal and professional success. By showing a genuine desire to get to know someone and seeking to help them, together with approaching life against the grain, you will grow immensely, with or without fancy titles or pedigree.

Give without the expectation of return, at least initially, and you'll be surprised. People have a built-in reciprocation point system, and they take note of what you do. I want to emphasize the importance of refraining from a quid pro quo mindset—at least in the first couple of interactions.

Of course, all relationships must have a symbiotic component, and failure to contribute by either party is sure to spell the end. If you're in a relationship where you find yourself always giving, giving, giving, and the other person is always taking, and shows little to no appreciation, then at some point you'll need to decide whether this relationship is worth your time and energy.

Tip: A great way to add value and make someone's day is to leave a review for them. This can be accomplished via Google reviews for their business or on websites like LinkedIn or Amazon. This approach requires minimal time and goes a long way towards building goodwill; it also enhances your visibility as other people will encounter your review. Now, imagine if you did this several times a week—leaving reviews for people and local businesses. You would help expand your reach immensely, thereby helping your business.

Picking Battles

While it's certainly appropriate at times to vocalize a grievance, pick and choose your battles wisely. Of course, life isn't as easy as pushing a button nor is it necessarily easy navigating the gray areas of everyday life. That said, do your best so as to protect your greatest asset: the people in your life.

How to Foster Relationships

Now that you've successfully established a new relationship, the next step is to nurture and further develop it. I suggest a multi-pronged approach. First, if you haven't done so already, be sure to add everyone to your various social media channels, such as LinkedIn, Instagram and whichever social platform is the latest and greatest. Your goal is to maintain a presence with that other person but do so while also providing them with enough room to breathe after you've met.

At the same time, reach out to a few people you haven't connected with in a while and ask how they're doing. Relationships, of course, require continuous maintenance, and investing of your time, energy and resources. For this reason, I encourage you to reach out, at the very least once a year, to all the contacts you value. If you don't do this, the relationship is likely to wither and if you eventually do need them, it may appear more transactional. If it has been a while since you've spoken with someone, especially if you only met them briefly at an event or in passing, they may not even remember you. So be sure to reference some aspect of your last conversation together. This is especially important on platforms like LinkedIn and Instagram, where

AI and automated messages have made it more challenging to determine whether a real human is messaging us. You might need to adjust your writing style so as to appear more human.

Again, do whatever you can to offer value to the person you're reaching out to. The more commonalities you can leverage, the more likely they are to bite. Perhaps you both attended the same university or enjoy a certain sports team.

Once you've connected, seek to build a symbiotic relationship with them. You may consider following up with a handwritten thank-you note. As you get to know them, figure out what's important to them. Maybe they're looking for a particular job, or they want to meet a prospective client. For the former, share their resume with a curated group. For the latter, set up an introductory call or group message between the two parties.

As your social media ecosystem grows, the next step is to begin inviting your contacts to curated social mixers (ideally, ones that you put together, but events you've been invited to work as well). For example, I could invite someone to the social group I co-founded, or to a private think tank I'm involved with as well. The key is always having a legitimate reason to reach out and offer value.

Relationship Management

Once you start to accumulate names and numbers on a mass scale, you'll need a way to keep track of everyone and store information about them. For many, customer relationship management (CRM) software is the way to go.

If you need a way to take down and keep track of copious notes and information for yourself or your team, then getting a CRM is ideal.

Believe it or not, as of this writing, I don't use a CRM. What I do instead is add notes to each of the contacts I have, which makes finding and recalling info easier. Some techniques I use include adding someone's picture to their contact information, writing their name phonetically if it's challenging to pronounce, adding a note about where or how I met them, and keeping track of some interesting facts or comments they made.

Sometimes, I organize individuals by where they live. For example, if I'm in Monaco, I can type "Monaco" in my contacts list and quickly identify all the contacts I have in that country.

I'm not too fond of business cards, as I feel they're yet another obstacle to getting your information into somebody's phone. In my opinion, the best way to exchange information is to send them your own digital contact card, which can be found at the very top of the contact list on your phone. Fill it out completely with all the information you want shared with people—including your photo, email, websites, social media, and phone number. Now, you can ask for people's phone numbers and then send this to them directly.

Now, they'll have everything they need to know about you in a format that won't get lost, crumpled up, dropped under the car seat, or left in a pocket and put through the wash.

Tip: Taking a picture with someone you just met can be a great way for both you and the other person to recall each other. Be sure to add their photo to their name when you input their contact information into your phone.

Social capital expert Judy Robinett, in her book *How to Be a Power Connector*, shares the value in triaging relationships strategically utilizing her 5+50+100 Rule. She illustrates this concept by using a three-tier model:

Top 5: Identify your Top 5 contacts and seek to engage and offer value to them on an almost daily basis. These contacts are ones that you would rely on with your life or are vital to your business.

Key 50: The Key 50 contacts are those that hold significant importance in your life. Be sure to handle these connections with care and continuously seek ways to contribute value to these relationships.

Vital 100: The Vital 100 are contacts in your Rolodex that you touch base with at least once a month. Again, seek to serve as a resource to this group of contacts.

You may consider adding a column to your 5+50+100 people by sorting their location, occupation and how they can be helped. This model will help not only with organizing these contacts, but it will force you to evaluate how you can be resourceful.

The Changing World

Our world is changing faster than ever before, both socially and technologically. Many of the jobs' people have today will inevitably be replaced by AI in the coming years. And those with careers centered around relationships will have the best chance of buoying the waters of change.

Awareness

As we meet and establish relationships, we don't always have the luxury, nor even the time, to thoroughly vet people. We must bear in mind that not all of the people we think of as our friends are indeed our friends. Many are only around so long as it's convenient or they think there's something to gain by associating with us. This applies to all forms of relationships, personal, professional or romantic.

Be friendly and cordial to everyone but keep your guard up until people prove themselves worthy.

Looking Out for Others

One of the things that's instilled when you serve in the military is the importance of looking after your people. It's hammered again and again in basic training and throughout a service member's career. If you're in the Navy, it's your swim buddy; in the Army, it's your battle buddy. Great emphasis is placed on always ensuring that you always have someone with you for safety, accountability and teamwork.

Outside of the military, there's far less oversight and sense of camaraderie. Today, people more or less have the notion that another's plight or problem isn't their business and doesn't affect them. While I'm all about minding one's business, there are times when it's appropriate to speak up and check in on people. Someone else's problems (i.e., drinking and driving, suicidal ideations, or relationship woes) could very easily become your problem or your organizations.

That's why I believe it's incumbent upon each of us to be proactive and check in on people. In the military, your inability to keep tabs on your "buddy" can lead to dire consequences. In the business world, issues don't tend to be as life-threatening. However, we're all interconnected. As seen throughout history, a single event can create a ripple effect that engulfs a community or the globe.

CHAPTER 7

HOSTING CURATED SOCIAL GATHERINGS

"Teamwork is the ability to work together toward a common vision. The ability to direct individual accomplishments toward organizational objectives. It is the fuel that allows common people to attain uncommon results."
– Andrew Carnegie

Why Host Social Affairs?

Because hosting curated social gatherings is one of the best ways to meet people, and it gives you a great reason to reach out to *anyone* you encounter. Who doesn't want to enjoy an evening at a beautiful estate or aboard a yacht? You can literally approach anyone, and, if you do so tactfully, you have a great reason to acquire somebody's contact information.

Moreover, they satisfy a deep human desire to connect and bond with others, in addition to positioning you and your partners as leaders and points of contact that people will naturally engage with before, during and after an event. In addition, they give you a great reason to reach out to anyone, especially when you're hosting an opulent experience that's of great intrigue.

Remember, especially in the post-pandemic world, people long for deeper social relationships, not simply "followers" on social media. (That said, we should make full use of social media to share our message and invite people to attend our curated experiences.)

An added advantage of hosting social gatherings is that they can give you an opportunity to enjoy high-ticket items without the need to own and maintain expensive assets—think mansions, yachts, private jets and exotic cars. With the help of business partners, you can fractionalize the investment needed to acquire these assets for your gatherings. And one of the best parts is—if done correctly—you can deduct these expenses for business purposes.

Moreover, orchestrating gatherings that offer a unique and interesting lifestyle also gives you a great platform for social media. The content that you create from these events will help to build your personal brand and engage with your audience, thereby channeling your followers towards your personal or professional objectives.

Finally, if you utilize an asset like a mansion or yacht, you may also meet the owners of these platforms and are likely to meet successful people in their sphere, ranging from neighbors to associates to friends.

There are a multitude of reasons as to why others will want to attend your social mixer, including:

- Meeting prospective clients
- An exciting experience to enjoy or share with friends
- Meeting a prospective romantic interest
- Experiencing a beautiful estate or yacht cruise
- Supporting a nonprofit organization
- Celebrating a holiday or accomplishment

The more of these needs you can satisfy, the better.

Note that when you host an event, it doesn't need to be some extravagant affair like you're from *The Great Gatsby*; it can be as simple as a small gathering at your home or a friend's place, or even at a restaurant. These events are meant to serve as a catalyst for creating a sense of community.

Furthermore, when you've successfully created a sense of belonging around these various activities for people, you'll naturally begin to generate interest. Ranging from vendors who may wish to offer their services to you, to include nonprofits that are seeking funding.

Now, if for any reason you can't host events yourself or with business partners, the next best option is to join an existing community and help them in some capacity. Ideally, position yourself as a gatekeeper—the one people must engage with in order to receive entry. However, this is the route most people take, and while it can certainly be rewarding, it's not as effective as being the host of an event you've helped orchestrate.

Another great reason for orchestrating social engagements is because when you create a social ecosystem that's both digital and in person—you've created something that's highly valuable to companies and business owners. That being your ability to influence an audience and direct attention to a given product or service. Now stop and think about how many companies pay millions of dollars each year on advertising so they can get in front of people— whether that's on platforms like Instagram or LinkedIn, or via golf events or music festivals. Now, if you're in business yourself, think of how lucrative it could be for you to have or run a social group.

Think of how vertically integrated such a platform could be. You have a product or service, or ideally you provide a whole host of services to the members of your social group—unlike your competitors who are paying hand over fist to various entities for marketing. As noted earlier, a tremendous void has been created by social media, remote work, and the decline of religion in people's lives, which has led to a real thirst for community and social engagement.

Additionally, crafting curated social affairs helps to stimulate the local economy by employing musicians, food and beverage vendors, photographers and a whole array of service professionals. You are in essence creating an ecosystem where many people stand to gain from the success of these events both personally and professionally.

Tip: You may consider creating a team or board of advisors to help facilitate in these curated affairs. I recommend, prior to doing so, to carefully vet any prospective individuals and ensure there isn't any potential for conflict.

Application

For example, let's say you run a software company and want to procure more business and/or stay in front of existing clients; you can host an event that brings all former and current clients together. If they're geographically spread out, consider hosting events of various sizes in various parts of the country throughout the year. This is where leveraging partners in other markets can come in handy.

You could even provide an online experience as an alternative option if you can't meet in person. However, I highly recommend that there be a strong incentive for people to engage online.

Geography & Hosting

Whether you're in a large city or a small town, whether you're on the coast, in the mountains or in a desert, there are always activities you can put together that leverage the environment you're in to create something unique and intriguing to your target audience.

What Type of Events Can I Host?

Aside from previously mentioned platforms such as yachts, mansions, jets, and exotic cars, you can conduct a 50 under 50 awards ceremony, a casino night, an art show or a tournament of some kind. The key is to try and offer an outlet for people that is atypical, something that gets people excited and talking about it.

However, I recommend refraining from most venues that are typically used to host social engagements, such as hotels, restaurants and country clubs, unless there's something very special about a particular one.

From my observation, many of the top business and sales books today don't cover the value in bringing people together, as a means to both expand your relationships and business efforts. The one common thread that does, however, appear to be mentioned is joining existing groups, which is beneficial; that said, it doesn't compare to spearheading one yourself or with business partners.

Finding Venues

There are a number of ways to find a place to meet, from securing a booking online via platforms such as Peerspace or Giggster to browsing short-term rentals or reaching out to your network or that of your social circle. If you're new to the area or have a smaller social circle, start by asking your work colleagues or neighbors. You can also reach out to people you interact with as you go about your day, such as at your favorite cafe or restaurant. Ideally, this will create synergy and leverage for you. Now, find a way to incentivize them to contribute in some capacity. Typically, business professionals are going to be the ones who are most open to collaborating, as many are seeking clients or customers for their product or service.

Personal story: When I first moved to Newport Beach, CA— I didn't know a soul. Instead of staying home, I would go out by myself in the evening to get out of the house and socialize. Now, I recognize that not everyone is inclined to go out by themselves, and if this is the case with you, I would encourage you to invite a colleague or date.

Event Financing

Once you've found a venue, you'll have to have a grasp of the economics—which can be quite the investment, depending on how extravagant you desire it to be. Aside from partnering with like-minded professionals as previously mentioned, consider reaching out to local businesses or corporations for sponsorship opportunities. This could be a capital contribution or the business offering their product or service.

Be creative; for instance, if you know the owner of a winery, you may offer to make them a sponsor in exchange for them providing several bottles of wine for your event. You can also reach out to real estate agents or mortgage brokers, who are typically aware of potential homes to serve as a venue—especially high-end homes. Properties that have been sitting on the market for a while are particularly attractive, because the owner and agent will probably be more inclined to help you as it will increase their exposure to prospective buyers.

Tip: A great way to get the owner of a mansion or yacht to consider allowing you to host is to figure out what's important to them—perhaps they have a business and they're seeking to get in front of people or perhaps they have a nonprofit that's near and dear to them. Once uncovered, leverage this knowledge to tailor your pitch to them. Perhaps you can help provide visibility for their business or nonprofit via an auction or raffle. You could make a banner, in addition to acknowledging their company on social media and verbally at the event. This is best achieved by sharing with the business owner and allowing them to imagine what they have to gain.

Moreover, I always advise my clients to compensate them in some capacity, whether it's a donation to them or a charity. Again, be sure to utilize every lever at your disposal.

This same technique can be applied to those with exotic cars, country club memberships and private jets. I always strive to structure opportunities creatively whenever possible, as it can help ensure that the numbers pencil.

So, there you have it; you know how to identify and ask for an opportunity to rent someone's home or yacht, how to finance and structure creatively with partners and how to position your value proposition.

My last comment is in regards to insurance, which I highly recommend, especially when conducting an event near any body of water such as a pool or aboard a yacht. We live in a litigious society, with opportunists seeking to enrich themselves, so be sure to protect yourself. However, don't go out of your way to advertise that you're using event insurance to the person you're renting from, unless they ask, as you could be taken advantage of for frivolous or nefarious purposes.

Vendors

Once you have the venue and insurance, the next step is to secure vendors. I recommend live music, hors d'oeuvres, and a bar with a competent bartender. Live music adds another dimension and creates a very different environment from simply playing music from someone's phone. Regarding food, hors d'oeuvres are perfectly acceptable, unless you really want to provide dinner. Offering dinner will significantly enhance the investment you make in the event and add additional logistical hurdles.

In seeking vendors, start by asking your existing contacts—friends, family, and co-workers. This both ensures quality and potentially gets you a friends and family rate. If this doesn't materialize, you'll have to scour the web for reviews of musicians, catering and beverage providers.

Charities

Aligning with a nonprofit can be an excellent move, especially when you're seeking to build goodwill in the community. This can also enhance the experience of the event, boost attendance, and reflect favorably on your organization, not to mention helping an important cause.

Equipment

If you plan on hosting at least once a month, I suggest buying any equipment you may need rather than renting it each time, as it will often pay for itself after a few uses. These items may include red carpet materials, stanchions, tables, chairs, linens, cocktail tables, and more.

Staffing

This can be a necessary expense, especially when you're hosting a large audience. First, consider bringing in valet services as well as a bathroom or coat attendant.

Another important consideration is security professionals. In addition to providing guests with a sense of safety, they can keep an eye out for any foul play that may arise. Moreover, it's easier for the security guard to turn someone away at the door or ask someone to leave. This way, you and your partners don't have to be the bad guy.

Neighbors

Be sure to invite the neighbors, when applicable. This serves a few purposes; first, it will build goodwill and notify them of your social gathering. Additionally, exchanging numbers is a great way to connect and communicate so as to ensure volume is within reason and any potential hiccups can be nipped immediately. There's nothing worse than having someone build up resentment only to unleash their fury on a matter that, if only addressed earlier, could have been amended. And for those with careers in the real estate or mortgage industry, this is a good legitimate reason to reach out to additional homeowners and offer value to them.

Tip: Decibel readers can be very effective for ensuring that volume levels are within city or HOA compliance. They can also help protect you from any fraudulent noise complaints, as you can record and capture the decibel range.

Planning Suggestions

Here are some options to consider for various aspects of the planning phase:

- **Venue** – Yacht, mansion, jet, waterfront house, cabin or desert oasis
- **Music** – Traditional or jazz band, classical music, or contemporary
- **Food** – Offer a variety of options, including vegan, non-allergenic, and shellfish free
- **Drinks** – Bartenders, drink instruments and equipment, supplies, ice and water
- **Raffle** or **Silent Auction** – Offering unique items or gift cards for nonprofits
- **Decor** – Exotic cars, champagne board, red carpet, stanchion and red rope, etc.
- **Security** – Ensure they appear professional and help with cleanup if need be
- **Payment Service** – Be sure to have credit card processing equipment or software
- **Logistics** – Luxury bus, limo, etc., to and from venue
- **Celebrities** – Influencers, prominent business people and/or local figures like politicians

- **Non-profit** – Kids, animals, medical or overseas charities
- **Marketing** – Website, social and print media, and news media coverage highlighting event
- **Team** and **Board of Advisors** – Be strategic with whom you bring aboard

Getting Guests

Once everything has been secured—venue, insurance, vendors, event equipment, etc.—the next step is to start sharing the news of your event. There's never been an easier time to share a message to a large audience, thanks to social media. Here are just a few of the many places you can share your upcoming event:

- Social media: posts, reels, stories and more
- Website
- Word of mouth
- Email & physical flyers
- Mailers
- Podcasts
- Radio
- Blog
- Local business journal
- Newspaper
- Magazines

We all know people who are "super connectors"—those in our communities who seem to know *everyone*. Be sure to invite these people and ask them to invite others they feel would add to the experience.

Work hard to have a good mix of genders—especially if you're hosting something like a yacht event. If you deliver in this area, people will sing songs about you till the end of time. If not, and this is your first event, it can be an uphill battle getting people to attend the next one, because people love to talk.

A website can also work wonders for your event, especially if you're intending to create a social group or make this a recurring event. Sites like Wix or Squarespace are easy and user friendly, and you can literally have a website up in under 36 hours. It doesn't need to be something incredibly sophisticated, with multiple pages and a painstaking design; to start with, it can be a one-pager that says "Coming soon..." and briefly shares the details of the event.

If you don't want to create your own website, you can utilize sites like Eventbrite; however, while this platform is easy to use, they take a significant cut of your earnings from ticket sales or sponsorships.

Sidenote: If you want to attract a top-shelf audience to your event—while still having admission open to the public—implement some form of vetting process, whether that's charging a certain amount or implementing a dress code.

Inviting Specific Guests

Often, there will be specific people you'll wish to invite but, for one reason or another, don't feel comfortable reaching out to directly. If this is the case, try inviting their friend or business associate instead, and allowing them to bring a guest. They will most likely mention your name in relation to the invite, thus helping you enter into the awareness of the person you wish to get in front of.

Private vs Ticketed Events

This choice depends to some degree on your budget, but I personally like offering tickets because it means attendees will have some skin in the game. When someone pays for a ticket, you'd better bet they'll make every effort to attend, especially if admission is pricey. When setting ticket prices, look at what other events are charging; calibrated of course, with what they're offering in comparison to you. The optimal price will also depend on your market and the clientele you're seeking to target.

Remember, you can always offer special rates or comped tickets for guests and/or sponsors.

Orchestration

If you have the budget, consider hiring an event specialist— or even better, having one as a business partner—to help ensure everything runs smoothly.

If, however, you're on a tight budget or want to do this yourself or with partners, consider the following:

- The viability of prospective partners
- Incorporating those with complementary skill sets to yours
- Including both men and women
- Allocation of expertise
- Choosing partners with substantial social reach

To illustrate, if you're more extroverted, consider adding somebody who is more introverted to run the behind-the-scenes aspect of your get-together such as running the finances or logistics. You may also consider partners who have existing relationships with food and beverage providers and local influencers, thereby helping to make the project more economical. And if you're setting out to create a social group, be sure to consider the long-term implications of a partnership that involves finances and any profit sharing.

Tip: If you're going to host a get-together yourself or with partners, remember to delegate and assign tasks, ensuring everyone has a role with well-defined expectations. Leveraging software can also make your life easier by allowing each person to keep track of who's completed what and ensuring timelines are being met.

Another suggestion, especially if you're seeking to preserve capital, is to acquire volunteers. These can be college students and/or professionals who are given access to the event for their help with set-up and take-down.

Finally, it's best to ensure in writing and with the approval of all decision-makers, so as to ensure without a shadow of a doubt that you have access to the platform on the big day. The last thing you want is for the owner of the estate or yacht to renege on the agreement last minute and leave you holding the bag. It's always better to over-communicate than under-communicate.

Preparing for Your Event

Now, if you've advertised your social event and haven't received very many RSVPs leading up to it, don't panic, as people tend to commit in the days leading up to the event. The key to incentivizing people to take action is to convey scarcity and incorporate a sense of urgency and FOMO (fear of missing out). If you're charging for tickets, then this may include increasing the price as the day of the event approaches.

By continuing to market your gathering and leveraging people of social clout, you'll help to galvanize interest and communicate the caliber of event.

Day of Event

Murphy's Law tells us that anything that can go wrong will go wrong. The various hiccups that I've encountered while hosting has been to be extra prepared and early. The last thing you want is to be too busy putting out fires to interact with your guests. That's why I encourage you to work with a team or, if it's in your budget, hire an event specialist to keep things running smoothly.

In any case, have things set up so that you can focus on entertaining your guests and ensuring everyone feels included in the festivities.

A good litmus test for an event that's going well is if people are staying at the venue and not migrating elsewhere. Including people sharing with you how much they're enjoying themselves.

Tip: Ensure that all valuables have been stored away and that bedrooms are locked. You'll also want to cover any tables or wood furniture to protect from damage. Rugs are another item to keep in mind. If possible, remove rugs because the last thing you want is a hefty bill because a Persian rug became soiled. Lastly, consider alternatives to red wine.

Post Event

You'll know the event was a success when people reach out to you the next day and thank you. You'll also see your social media feed light up with people talking about how great their evening was. When done right, an event can *significantly* expand your presence. All of this exposure you receive can then be channeled towards your personal or business endeavors.

Now, give yourself a short break, then immediately begin triaging the next steps and what could have been improved.

Depending on what experience you're looking to provide and how often, you may wish to segue into a private members-only club—this is to ensure that the right people are attending your events. (If, God forbid, the social experiences you're providing begin to veer off course, you must intervene immediately to avoid running aground.) Of course, if you go this route, be sure to set up the appropriate legal documentation to establish roles and set expectations.

As your group expands in size, expect your events to gain more and more traction, with more businesses becoming interested in sponsorship opportunities. At some point, it may behoove you to expand to other markets and open up businesses that compliment the social group you've created.

Additional Revenue Sources

Congrats—you've created a community around the events you've put together! And you've met a great deal of people in the process, by helping them connect with others. Now you may or may not be offering tickets, but either way, you can explore other business ventures in connection with this newfound community.

Perhaps you can offer an exclusive item to members, or white label a beverage or another product or service. You may even consider creating a mobile app for your users to engage with one another. Paid memberships are another option if you can put together consistent events. You now possess incredibly valuable social capital, and the avenues to monetize it are endless. If you can make these events a monthly staple, you'll grow tremendously, both personally and professionally.

Steps to Host

Step 1: Solo vs Collaboration

Determine whether you're doing this yourself or with partners. Working with others can help ensure the event is both successful and economically viable.

Step 2: Purpose & Target Audience

Start out by considering where you are, where the people you hope to connect with are, and what you know about your target audience. What age range are they? Who are they culturally, religiously and politically? What are their interests? What do they crave? And then what's your objective in communicating with them? Are you an investment banker seeking to build relationships with a sophisticated demographic, or perhaps an artist who wishes to connect with fellow artists or patrons? What are you offering them that's of value?

Step 3: Platform

As previously espoused, here are prospective venue ideas:

- Mansion
- Beachfront house
- Lake house
- Cabin
- Yacht
- Lake boat
- Underutilized commercial building

I highly recommend picking venues that most people aren't exposed to and/or wouldn't otherwise get to experience everyday; something incredible and mesmerizing. Remember, you want to satisfy as many areas of their interest as possible so as to whet their appetite.

Step 4: Advertising

Leverage as many social media platforms as you can, and consider teaming up with people who complement you, have the ability to bring in sponsorship proceeds, secure venues and reach a large audience though their network.

Six of the most important social media channels as of this writing are:

- Instagram
- TikTok
- Facebook

- LinkedIn
- X
- YouTube

The late rock musician Jim Morrison said, *"Whoever controls the media, controls the mind."* Leverage your gatherings to create media content that captures the imagination of others and directs viewership towards your objectives.

Influencers

Don't be afraid to reach out to local influencers, like community leaders, business magnates and celebrities. Offer them something in exchange for them sharing your event with their followers, like a comped ticket for them and a guest, and/or commission with each ticket they sell. You can also offer to purchase their product or service and offer it at your event. This can be illustrated in the celebrity with a wine or beverage they wish to market.

Step 5: Implementation

On the day of the event, focus on delivering an exceptional experience for your guests.

Step 6: Rinse, Recycle & Repeat

If this is something you enjoy doing, and you see the value in it, then explore event number two and repeat the process. You may even consider creating a website and social media account, in addition to setting up your group as an official entity.

Final Words

Over the course of this book, we've explored several topics pertaining to building authentic relationships. We've examined the importance of your mental and physical state; the optics that you present to the world both digitally and in person; the basics of persuasion; and unconventional ways to connect and build relationships, with curated social gatherings being amongst the best vehicles. Remember, you don't need to reinvent the wheel; leverage existing knowledge by seeking counsel from others and by emulating those who have found success in what they do. As practice makes perfect, I encourage you to continually refine your EQ skills each day. In the words of the late Zig Ziglar, *"Repetition is the mother of learning."* It's one thing to read a book or have great knowledge; it's another to actually apply the information in real life. I wish you the best in your journey and look forward to hearing from you.

APPENDIX

The books mentioned below have served me well, and I highly recommend each one of them. If you don't have the time to sit down and read, try listening to the audio versions as you work out or drive. You can also save time by speeding up the narration.

Recommended Books

- How to Win Friends and Influence People by Dale Carnegie
- How to Master the Art of Selling by Tom Hopkins
- The 48 Laws of Power by Robert Greene
- Think and Grow Rich by Napoleon Hill
- The Power of Positive Thinking by Norman Vincent Peale
- Influence: The Psychology of Persuasion by Robert Cialdini
- The Closers Survival Guide by Grant Cardone (I recommend the audio version)
- The Art of War by Sun Tzu

- How to be a Power Connector by Judy Robinson
- Networking to Get Customers, a Job or Anything You Want by Chris Haroun

Military Lessons

The following are lessons I learned while serving in the Navy:

- Don't just pull your weight, give as much as you can for your team (within reason).
- Strive to always be prepared and early.
- Train hard, so when you have to do the real thing it's not nearly as taxing.
- What can go wrong, will go wrong—so be prepared.
- Perception is reality.
- Embrace the ebb and flow of life; remain stoic.
- Take complete ownership of everything.
- Ultimately, desire is the catalyst behind all accomplishments.

Health Routine

Here's my routine for optimal mental and physical health:

- Exercise at least a few times a week—to include both cardio and weightlifting.
- Take natural herbal supplements if necessary.
- Go on walks as often as you can.
- Stay hydrated throughout the day.

- Meditate and incorporate breathing exercises during anxious times.
- Strive for a healthy diet each day.

Success Exercises

The following is my routine:

- Visualization (Done both in the AM & PM while listening to frequency music.)
- Write goals as if you've already accomplished them (AM & PM).
- State your goals aloud, as if you've already achieved them (AM & PM).
- Vision boards (Turn your computer wallpaper or room into images of your objectives.)
- Dress and look sharp (When you look good, you feel good, and people respond in kind.)

My Favorite Quotes

- "If you make a sale, you can earn a commission. If you make a friend, you can earn a fortune." —Jeffery Gitomer
- "Three may keep a secret, if two of them are dead." —Benjamin Franklin
- "You have power over your mind—not outside events. Realize this, and you will find strength." —Marcus Aurelius

- "We are what we repeatedly do. Excellence is not an act, but a habit." —Aristotle
- "Be careful whom you associate with. It is human to imitate the habits of those with whom we interact. We inadvertently adopt their interests, their opinions, their values, and their habit of interpreting events." —Epictetus
- "A man is but the product of his thoughts, what he thinks he becomes." —Mahatma Gandhi
- "Life is what happens to us while we are making other plans." —Allen Saunders
- "The strongest negotiating position is being able to walk away and mean it." —Corey Wayne
- "Courage isn't having the strength to go on—it is going on when you don't have strength." —Napoleon Bonaparte

For more insights visit christian's website:
www.christianwhite.me

ABOUT THE AUTHOR

Christian White

Possessing a multifaceted background, Christian White is an entrepreneur, coach, and consultant. He's also a veteran and a co-founder of social groups in Newport Beach and Beverly Hills, California. Actively engaged in his community, Christian has provided guidance and consultancy to numerous individuals in the fields of social capital and client acquisition. Hailing from Central California, he has a deep appreciation for military history, enjoys golf, and relishes outdoor activities. He resides in Newport Beach, California.

Made in United States
Troutdale, OR
12/10/2023

15604514R00076